ROGER JONES

FREESTYLE WINDSURFING

A Roger Jones Production

RJ

FREESTYLE WINDSURFING

ROGER JONES

HARPER & ROW, PUBLISHERS

SAN FRANCISCO

1817

Cambridge   London
Hagerstown   Mexico City
Philadelphia   São Paulo
New York   Sydney

Freestyle can be a lot of fun.

ACKNOWLEDGEMENTS

Design: John Clemmer
Text editor: Penny Caldwell
Photosequence Layout concepts:
Roger Jones
Front cover photo: Alan Williams
Inside color photographs: Alastair
Black, Alan Williams
Black and white photographs: Roger
Jones, Alan Williams, Chris Doroz,
Tarcisia Khomasurya
Technical advisors: Alan Adelkind,
Derek Wulff

NOTE

Technically, 'windsurfing' refers to sail-
ing Windsurfer-brand products, and
sailing other brands is 'boardsailing'.

Library of Congress Cataloging in Publication Data

Jones, Roger B.
  Freestyle windsurfing with Gary Eversole.
  Includes Index.
  1. Windsurfing. I. Eversole, Gary. II. Title.
  GV811.63. W56J66   1983   797.1'72   82-48931
  ISBN 0-06-250725-7

83 84 85 86 87 10 9 8 7 6 5 4 3 2 1

CONTENTS

Roger Jones is an experienced boardsailor and author. He conceived and co-authored The Wind is Free/ Windsurfing *with Ken Winner, and has written articles for magazines in Europe and North America on every aspect of the sport.*

PREFACE

Freestyle is a marvelous, beautiful gift of chance, a melding of sailing, ballet, gymnastics and self-expression which the inventors of the sailboard never dreamed possible. As fascinating to watch as to do, it's an activity every boardsailor can participate in, and anyone who has the idea that it's primarily for those who perform for competition couldn't be more wrong. If anything, the reverse is true; all over the world you'll find boardsailors performing helicopters, railrides and many other tricks purely for pleasure. Freestyle is for all who love the unique harmony of wind, water, boat and skipper that lies at the heart of boardsailing.

Roger Jones

USING THE BOOK

For easy access I've divided the contents list into Body Tricks, Board Tricks, Body & Sail Tricks, Riding the Rail and Reverses. At the end of the book is a glossary explaining key terms as they are used in the text.

You'll probably gain most from the book if you first skim through to get an idea of what is in it. Don't hesitate to jump directly to sections that particularly interest you, because you'll progress fastest when your attention is fully engaged.

Wherever possible I've grouped together tricks which are related; for example, those involving sailing clew-first. I've also tried to organize the book so each basic move is described before it is included in a complex sequence or combination trick.

Study the illustrations closely to understand where

the wind is, and estimate the direction and magnitude of the forces on the board, the rig, and the skipper.

As you read, go through the motions with an imaginary board and sail. Later, practice on the beach with a rig, perhaps with the board, too.

I've tried to highlight some of the fundamental moves in freestyle. Once you've physically understood them and know which moves flow best from one to another, then you're ready to develop your own combinations, even invent your own tricks.

Finally, bear in mind that this is a guide to help you develop your own technique, not an inflexible account of how you must do certain tricks. Freestyle is as personal as your signature.

ADVICE FROM GARY EVERSOLE

There are certain steps you can take to make learning freestyle easier. First, familiarize yourself with the forces acting on the rig. A few maneuvers on the beach, as described in the next chapter, will make clear the position of the center of effort in the sail, the balance point on the boom, and the angle you must incline the rig to balance it.

Next, I recommend that each time you start a new trick you figure out where the sail will be at each stage and the forces that will be involved. The idea is to learn how to use these forces to your advantage. Good freestyle uses technique, not strength.

Accept, at the outset, that learning is time-consuming. It took me six weeks at about 20 hours a week to learn a basic railride. That's 120 hours for one trick. However, it probably won't take you as long. Freestyle has advanced so far that it's much easier for people beginning now—not only because you can watch others and take advice, but because just knowing that a move is

Know which tricks you can do and the conditions in which they can be successfully performed.

Gary Eversole has won numerous American and international freestyle titles. Recognized as one of the world's most knowledgeable and innovative free-stylists, he has established many new tricks including the backflip through the boom (1979 Windsurfer World Championships), the everoll (1979), and a pirouette on the rail (1980).

possible puts you ahead of the person who hasn't heard of it. In the early days, there was nobody around to show us the way, or tell us what was possible.

Learning also requires intense concentration. Therefore, if you're working on a difficult maneuver, spend an hour on it each day while you're fresh, then move on to something different. You'll progress faster and have more fun that way.

Developing new tricks

People often ask how I develop new tricks. That's a difficult question to answer. For a while I discovered a new trick every few months. Then, two years into my boardsailing, that stopped happening, and for some time I thought I probably wouldn't come up with any more. It took a year before I hit anything new. So sometimes it seems as if you either hit or you don't, and there's little you can do about it.

One thing I'm sure is essential: you must think about what you are doing. Then, when you get into a predicament, when something unforeseen happens, try to work out how to handle the forces that caused the situation. If the rig or the board wants to go a certain way, let it go, flow with it. This way, you may end up stumbling onto new tricks... new to you anyway; later on you may find that someone else already discovered them.

For example, I discovered the everoll while practicing gybes. The board wanted to turn over as I gybed, so I learned how to let it turn over and still stay on it, and there was the everoll.

Creating variations on existing tricks is easier. That can often be done by listing all the tricks you know and mentally going through them, searching for combinations, small alterations and so on. With 10 tricks in your repertoire, you can combine and vary them almost endlessly.

Competitive freestyle

Basic guidelines

When you enter a competition it's important to find out what the other competitors can do, so you know what you must do to win. It's also important to find out what the judges are looking for. Try to assess their points allocation system. Find how much you are penalized for errors such as a fall or a sail drop, and weigh the risk of doing a difficult move against the potential gain.

Remain confident of your ability, but don't get into situations where you risk falling. Never try a trick in competition that you can't do successfully eight times out of 10 in practice sessions. If conditions aren't ideal, perform a conservative routine. Others may do more original and difficult tricks, but if they fall and you stay on your board, you have a good chance of winning. While the judges are looking for originality, they're also assessing how smoothly you flow from one trick to another and how gracefully you do each trick.

Never execute standard sailing moves in your routine. When you tack or gybe, add something to make it

different, a spin or pirouette for example. Arrange your tricks so the board doesn't stop moving and then have to be re-started. Stopping looks particularly bad in lighter wind.

Most competitions have three-minute routines. Be careful how you use this time. I've seen people spoil their chances by performing a good routine for 2½ minutes, then, on receiving their ½-minute warning, trying something so difficult that they fall. In a freestyle routine, 30 seconds is a long time. On receiving the warning continue your normal routine, counting until you reach 25 seconds. With five seconds to go, perhaps try for something difficult and spectacular. Depending on the judges' points system, a fall at the end may not be as damaging as a fall in the middle of the routine. If points are awarded for dismounts, see if you can turn the spill into a dismount.

Creating a routine

Design a routine that keeps you within 50 feet and on the same side of the sail as the judges. Stay where they can see as much as possible as easily as possible.

I do my tricks within an imaginary square, staying

Nosewalk reverse helicopter (above).

within this small area even during practice.

Select tricks that enable you to spend equal time on each side of the board, and develop them so you can do them on either tack. If you learn first on the side that comes hardest, the other side will come almost naturally.

Variety

Your choice of tricks should impart freshness and variety to the routine. Allow five seconds for each trick—no longer—and develop a repertoire that takes more than three minutes to complete. This way, if you go faster than planned or leave anything out, you won't have to repeat a trick.

Start the routine with at least 20 relatively simple moves, a sail 360, board 360, ducktack, back-to-back, helicopter and so on. Then begin performing progressively more difficult moves.

Psyching up for competition

It's important to relax when you're performing. I find it best to go out about 15 minutes ahead of time and be sailing when I'm called up.

You'll feel more confident if you have a large reper-

toire, then you can put together a routine to suit any situation you find yourself in.

Improvising versus planning your routine

My approach relies more on spontaneity than on a planned routine. I like to be free-flowing, do whatever happens, whatever feels good.

I do plan a few tricks to start off my routine. But after that I prefer to improvise. To do this you must be proficient at a large number of tricks and know many ways to combine them.

This system works well for me, but it may not work for everyone. Some people need more formalized routines, more conscious planning. Stick to whatever works best for you.

Keep in mind, though, that you'll likely have to decide spontaneously when to include very difficult tricks in your routine—a backflip on the rail, for example—because such moves require that conditions be just right.

•

Above all, I'd advise people who want to be good freestylists to go out and practice a lot, and enjoy it like I always have. That's what it's all about.

Practice each trick for a short time while you're fresh, then move on to something different ...

GETTING STARTED

Preparing Yourself

Learning is more satisfying if you feel you are progressing well. With this in mind, the following checklist compiles the suggestions of several top freestylists, including Gary Eversole, Ken Winner and Lisa Penfield.

Understand

Make sure you fully understand the sequence of movements and are ready for the forces they will unleash.

Concentrate

Though you must concentrate, avoid grim jaw-locked determination. If you focus on the trick, yet remain relaxed and open to feedback from the process of doing it, new insights will occur to you.

Be confident

Believe you are capable of the trick, otherwise you won't be fully committed to the effort it takes.

Be flexible

Remain open to spontaneous changes of plan and you'll save lots of falls. Be ready to convert an unmanageable force into one you can handle. Luff the sail, get out of its way, grab the mast, boom or board—do whatever will save you.

Be tenacious

Don't be discouraged by temporary failure. Those polished performances of today's experts result from hundreds of failed attempts. Remember, learning what to do also involves learning what not to do, so even a fall can have positive value.

Picture and plan in advance

Imagine the trick before trying it, and when refining your performance. Mentally go through the movements, even flex your muscles the way you would during the trick. This way, the maneuver will come to you more easily on the water. Such imaginary or 'inner' freestyle is possible almost anywhere, and is especially effective just before going to sleep.

Seek appropriate conditions

Shallow, flat water is best. Light wind is suitable for learning some tricks such as helicopters. Then, in higher wind, all you have to do is learn how to accentuate your movements and lean the rig farther to windward. However, other tricks (railrides; a head dip) are easier in moderate wind.

Loosen up

Do some stretching exercises before going onto the water. Keep arms, waist, belly and legs supple. In addition, be aware that some tricks call for special suppleness.

Observe others and take advice

Watch experts for what to do and watch the inexpert for what to avoid. If you know someone more advanced than you, ask for advice.

Learn in progressive stages

Many maneuvers can be most easily mastered by breaking them down into separate learning stages.

Identify problems systematically

If you have a persistent problem, stop and seek its cause. Is it merely tiredness? Or is water inside your ear impairing balance? Could it be you've failed to understand something? Sit on the board and review what you've been doing. Having identified the problem, relax and focus yourself on the trick. When you're ready, get up and try again.

Preparing Your Equipment

It is especially important that your equipment be reliably and tightly held together. In particular, the mast base must not pop out of the board unexpectedly, and the mast-boom connection must not flop around and ruin your precision.

It's also essential that your feet don't slip on the board. That means you'll need light footwear that grips extremely well, and/or you'll have to roughen the surfaces where you need good traction.

Masts used for railrides and everolls should be reinforced with fiberglass tape and epoxy resin, as illustrated in my book, Windsurfing with Ken Winner. Reinforce where the booms attach and at the mast base.

Understanding The Forces on the Rig

Locate the balance point of the boom

As Gary Eversole has said, one of the first things to do is locate the center of effort of the sail and the balance point of the boom. The center of effort is the point through which all forces on the sail can be considered to act. The balance point on the boom results from the action of the sail's force at either end of the boom.

Choose a day with steady, light to moderate wind, and wedge the mast foot into sand or grass. Sheet in and find the point on the boom at which it can be held with one hand without the rig swinging off one way or the other. This is the balance point, the point at which the forces exerted fore and aft balance each other. In most sails the center of effort is slightly above the balance point of the boom.

Use the balance point to pivot the rig

Hold the boom, with your hands an equal distance on either side of the balance point. Spin the rig around the balance point in a mast-to-leeward direction by relaxing strain on the forward hand and pulling in with the aft hand. Then, backwind the sail and spin the rig around the other way, clew to windward, by pushing with the aft hand while reducing pressure on the forward hand. Though it may seem trivial now, using the forces in the sail to pivot the rig around the balance point is one of the most important techniques you will learn at this stage.

Balance the rig

Luff the sail and incline the mast to windward until the rig balances when you take both hands off. Note the mast angle. In stronger wind, the mast must be leaned farther to windward than this.

Straight arms give more power

Many freestyle moves are best performed by holding the boom with arms extended, not bent. This gives you more power and more room to move around the rig.

Extended arms also reduce the unpredictability of freestyle because, unless your arms stretch, you always know how far away the rig is and so can build up reliable habit-reactions.

When you feel you've understood these basic concepts, get started with some tricks. Let the fun begin.

With the sail full, find the balance point on the boom so precisely that you can hold the rig with just one finger.

Splits while sailing clew-first, by U.S. freestyle champion Lisa Penfield. Loosen up onshore before attempting such tricks.

1 Inside the boom

Inside the boom is demonstrated by American freestyle champion Lisa Penfield. It's a good trick to begin freestyle with because it's fairly easy in a moderate, steady wind.

Sail on a close reach. Sheet out. Then put your forward hand on the mast and incline it slightly to windward. Slide your rear hand inside the boom, duck your body inside, and sheet in with your rear hand.

Once you're sailing a steady course, lean back and put your weight on the rig. By positioning your back astride the balance point, you can release with both hands and use just your shoulders.

Of course, there are more showy ways to get inside the boom. You can luff, tilt the rig far enough to windward to balance it, then let go with both hands, duck inside and sheet in with your back.

Handling gusts

When a gust hits, sheet out by twisting your rear shoulder to leeward, and at the same time tilt the mast slightly farther to windward.

The first few times a gust pulls you forward you may have to make a conscious effort to overcome the natural impulse to pull against it. Pulling back only puts you in deeper trouble by putting yet more power in the sail.

2 | Neck hold

Physiotherapists don't recommend the neckhold. It isn't difficult, but try it only in light wind, and only for a short time.

Sailing on a beam reach, sheet out and duck your head inside the boom, retaining hold with both hands while you position the boom across one shoulder and between your neck and back. The idea is to take part of the strain with your back.

Gradually slacken your hands off the boom, making sure the rig is perfectly balanced before taking both hands away.

To return to normal sailing, simply bend your head down and catch the boom as it slides off.

3 | Hand drag

This maneuver can be added to a freestyle routine very quickly if the time seems right.

Simply hold the boom at the balance point while you release the rear hand and bend your knees to get close to the water.

4 | Facing lee side of sail

One way to put yourself on the lee side of the sail is by tacking without changing sides. When tacking, push strongly with the rear foot while you oversheet the sail, pulling it across the board's midline to turn the bow well onto the new tack.

As you steer away from the wind, facing the lee side, you may have to luff to avoid being thrust off the front of the board. Standing on one leg, the way Lisa Penfield does here, is a good example of how flair can be imparted to a relatively simple trick.

5 | Pirouette

A pirouette is most easily performed on a close reach. Luff the sail and tilt the rig to windward until it balances. Then, release with both hands, spin on one foot, and catch the boom again before the rig has time to move.

When you release the boom do so cleanly. To set yourself spinning, throw your arms across your chest as you push off with one foot. The closer you bring your arms to your chest the faster you'll spin. Stand straight or you'll rotate off the board and into the water.

In the illustration, Gary has spun toward the wind by spinning on his forward foot. Some freestylists, Ken Winner for example, prefer turning in the opposite direction and therefore spin on the rear foot.

6 | Walkaround

A walkaround is similar to a pirouette but is done in several steps. The appeal of a pirouette lies in its grace and speed, whereas a walkaround can be used to generate suspense, especially if you turn in slow motion, using seven or eight tiny steps.

Proceed much as for a pirouette. Luff, balance the rig, release with both hands, and then walk around.

If you prefer not to release the rig for the entire turn, you can hold it with one hand over your shoulder, then release and throw the hand around to catch the boom again a split second later.

Leeward boom bite.

indward boom bite.

7 | Dentists' delight

The dentists' delight, otherwise known as a boom bite, is a light-air trick which may look funny but can give extra points in competition. Besides, there's nothing wrong with putting humor into freestyle.

The windward boom bite requires very light wind and can only be done for a moment, depending on how strong your mouth is—and how large it is.

You're not trying to bite the boom so much as to push down on it. Hook your head over and inside the boom so it lifts into your jaws.

The leeward boom bite is easier because, being on the lee side of the sail, you can put one leg against the mast and the other against the sail. In this position you could in fact release the boom with your mouth and push your chest against it.

8 | Head dip

The head dip is best learned in steady wind of about 10 to 12 knots.

Sailing on a close reach, bend your knees to bring your body in over the board. Then, hang your weight down on the rig and sheet out a little, arching your back and stretching your neck back to reach the water.

As well as dipping your head into the water, try sailing along looking at the world upside down.

There is a tendency for the board to head up as you do a head dip. Compensate by bearing off slightly as you begin, and avoid tilting the rig aft as you stretch back.

In lighter winds, you may have to drop the forward hand low on the mast for support, to take advantage of the increased leverage.

When the wind is far too light to hold you, it's still possible to do a head dip by positioning your knees under the sail and over the lee side of the board, as Ken Winner does here. This way, you can hang your weight vertically down through the mast. If necessary, you can even drop your rear hand to the foot of the sail.

Gary Eversole does a head dip in moderate wind.

Lighter wind head dip by Ken Winner.

Splits with a head dip by Lisa Penfield.

9 | Splits with head dip

Before attempting this combination trick you should already be able to do the splits on a sailboard.

Sail on a close reach. If your boom is high, drop the forward hand onto the mast while the other hand holds the boom.

Slide your front foot about three feet forward of the mast. Then, slide your rear foot back until you are in the splits, the front leg pointing forward, the back leg making about a 45° angle with the front leg.

For the head dip, arch your back considerably and stretch your neck back. If the wind is light, you'll probably have to put your forward hand quite low on the mast and hold the foot of the sail with the other hand, as Lisa Penfield does in the illustration.

There's a tendency for the board to turn towards the wind during this trick. Watch the sail and, if the board comes so close to the wind that the sail luffs, throw the rig forward to bear off. Don't bear off so much that you have more power in the sail than you can handle. In fact, if the wind is strong it's a good idea that the sail luff a bit so it exerts less force.

In strong wind, the board may head up very rapidly, so complete the maneuver quickly.

To stand up again, slide both feet together quickly. If there's enough wind you'll be pulled into a sitting position. From there, just stand up. If the wind is light, keep your weight acting vertically down through the rig as you pull yourself up.

10 | Boom stepover

Long-legged people find this trick a breeze. It's quite versatile and can be done by starting from inside and stepping over to outside, or vice versa. For example, you could start from normal sailing, from a back-to-back, or from inside the boom with your back to the windward side of the sail.

To do a stepover, bring the board head-to-wind, luff, and tilt the rig as far back as you can, even dipping the clew into the water if that's necessary to get the boom low enough for you.

Step over the boom very quickly while the board passes through the eye of the wind. Avoid stepping too far aft or you'll sink the tail. Once over the boom throw the rig forward, catch the wind, and bear off.

11 | Forward windward foothold

Many footholds are possible. They aren't all action-packed, but can still be fun to try. Light to moderate wind is needed for this one.

Sail normally, then turn around to face the stern. To turn around without releasing both hands at the same time, first reach the rear hand across your body to grasp the mast with a thumb-down grip. Then release the other hand and turn around in one smooth movement.

Sit down, sliding the forward hand

12 | Forward leeward foothold

This light-air trick is the foothold equivalent of facing the lee side of the sail.

In the illustration Doug Wilson of Ontario, Canada lies forward of the mast while sailing forward. Because the wind is so light he supports the sail with his left foot. Had there been a little more wind he'd have placed both feet on the lee side of the rig.

13 | Stern-first foothold

For simplicity I've put the stern-first foothold with the other footholds, though properly it belongs in a section of 'body and board' tricks.

This trick is done while running stern first in very light wind, the skipper lying to leeward of the sail.

If you start from normal sailing, first bring the board head-to-wind, then turn your back to the sail and back-wind it so as to sail stern first downwind.

Next, sit down, lowering the rig over yourself and sliding one hand down the mast, the other hand down to the foot of the sail.

Once you are lying down, put your feet up to the boom and push it away, bracing yourself against the board.

down the mast and the other hand down to the foot of the sail. Control sail trim and course as necessary. Once you raise your feet to the boom you should be able to release both hands and control the rig with just the soles of your feet.

14 | Spin tack

For this type of spin tack the skipper spins 180° as the board is tacked. In my book *Windsurfing with Ken Winner* I illustrated a different spin tack in which the skipper spins the opposite way, resulting in a 540° rotation.

Sailing close-hauled, lean the mast aft and head up, stepping one foot forward of the mast and putting the forward hand on the mast (frame 1).

When the board is head-to-wind, luff, lean the rig forward (frame 2), and pass the mast from hand to hand as you spin (frames 2, 3 and 4). Step aft on the new side, sheet in and bear off on the new tack.

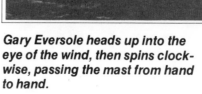

Gary Eversole heads up into the eye of the wind, then spins clockwise, passing the mast from hand to hand.

Once you've tried this a few times, experiment with different hand movements. For example, see if you can eliminate the first hand change (forward hand to mast) and still spin smoothly. That is to say, when the board is head-to-wind, leave the forward hand on the boom, and reach across your body with the rear hand to grip the mast with the thumb down.

For something completely different, when the board comes head-to-wind transfer the forward hand to the mast above your head. Then spin 180° beneath this hand, throw the mast forward, and catch it with the other hand (the new forward hand) as you step into normal sailing position.

Give some thought to other possibilities; practice on land, and see what you can come up with. As always, do whatever works best for you.

3

4

5

15 | Spin gybe

To do a spin gybe, first gybe the board into clew-first sailing, then spin a full revolution while allowing the clew to flip over the bow into normal sailing position.

The text below describes how to effect the transitions between each frame of the photosequence. **Frames 1-2** Gybe the board but don't let the sail pass over the bow. Rather, broad-reach clew-first for a moment on the new tack. **Frames 2-3** Next, release the hand nearest the clew, pull the mast to windward and, as the sail swings over the bow, spin your body around the opposite way, grabbing the mast with your free hand. The purpose of pulling the mast to windward is to compensate for the momentum of the rig swinging to leeward. **Frames 3-4** Keeping a firm hold on the mast, release the hand that remained on the boom and complete your spin in time to catch the other boom. Sheet in for normal sailing.

1. Gybe the board.

2. On the new tack, broad-reach clew-first for a moment.

Troubleshooting

If you find the board heads up too rapidly as you spin, it could be because you move too far back on the board, or because you lean the mast aft. In order to keep the mast more upright and stand farther forward on the board, you may have to experiment with alternative hand transitions, and delay your spin until the clew has already swung across the bow and dissipated some of its momentum.

4. Catch the boom and head up on the new tack.

3. Spin 360° as you let the sail flip over the bow.

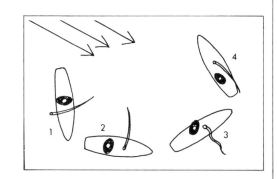

16 | Back-to-front hang-out

On the basis that sailing with your back to the lee side of the sail is called a back-to-back, perhaps an appropriate name for sailing with your back to the windward side of the sail is a back-to-front hang-out.

Canadian boardsailor Derek Wulff demonstrates one method of getting into position.

Sailing on a close reach, he luffs and steps forward, transferring his rear hand to the mast, thumb down. This turns his body partway around (frame 3).

To complete his turn he releases the hand still on the boom (4), turns and puts it aft on the boom (5).

When he sheets in he leans forward, bracing his foot against the mast step.

Some freestylists prefer the back-to-front hang-out with both hands on the boom. If you do it this way, it's probably easier to transfer the rear hand directly to the boom at the outset.

Handling gusts

It's difficult to pull really hard against the rig in the back-to-front position. So even as you pull, be prepared to luff by twisting at the waist and shoulders if you feel you are being pulled backwards. If you get pulled into an arched-back position you may have to release the boom with the rear hand. Then, before sheeting in again, incline the mast farther to windward.

1. Sail on a close reach and luff.

4. Release the boom.

2. Step forward and transfer your rear hand to the mast, thumb down.

3. You are now turned halfway around.

5. Complete the turn by reaching swiftly around to grab the boom well aft.

6. Brace your forward foot against the mast step and lean forward as you sheet in.

17 Back-to-front inside the boom

This is probably easiest on a close reach, though the illustration shows a more downwind course.

One way to get into position is by first crossing your hands on the boom, selecting an underhand grip for the hand that you move forward. This enables you to duck inside and turn around without releasing the boom in the process. Try it and you'll see what I mean.

An alternative is to release with the rear hand, duck inside and turn, having first moved the forward hand slightly nearer the clew, again using an underhand grip.

Sailing back-to-front inside the boom isn't very difficult, and is possible even in strong wind, once you learn how to sheet out in the gusts. It's no use pulling against gusts, because you'll only end up being pulled backwards.

18 Nose dip

Once you can sail back-to-front you can try a nose dip. A lower boom makes this easier, as does steady moderate wind.

A nose dip in almost zero wind is shown here. Kneel down, sliding your forward hand down the mast, and grasp the foot of the sail with the other hand. Balance the rig and hold it vertical. Bring your body as close to the board as you can, and support your weight by pulling vertically down through the rig.

Moderate and strong wind technique

Sail back-to-front, hanging outside the boom. Lean well out, step aft to bring the boom nearer the water, and slowly tilt the rig as far to windward as you can without pulling it entirely over. You'll really have to stretch to reach the water.

1

3

4

5

3. Grab the boom again and head up.

19 | Pirouette gybe

In a pirouette gybe the rig is released with both hands, whereas for a spin gybe one hand always holds the rig. Thus a pirouette gybe is best in light wind, while a spin gybe is still possible in moderately strong wind.

As you gybe, lean the mast aft to balance the rig. Then release it, pirouette quickly, and grab the rig before it blows away.

2. As the board turns onto the new tack, lean the rig aft until it balances. Then release and pirouette.

1. Gybe the board.

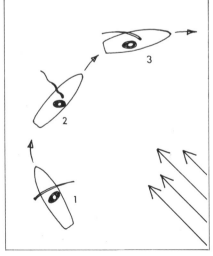

20 | Board 360

To do a board 360, rotate the hull through one complete revolution while the sail remains full above it.

This maneuver is initiated by leaning the rig back as if to tack. When the hull reaches head-to-wind, keep the sail full on the original tack and use your feet to push the hull around beneath it.

When you start the second half of the turn, and the board turns downwind, you'll probably have to sheet out slightly so the rig doesn't pull you forward.

For sailors who enter regattas there's a practical side to this trick—if someone protests you during a race you can do a board 720 on the course without losing much time. It's possible to keep the board moving forward throughout a 360; therefore, it's often faster in the long run to complete the first full turn, then sail on a short way and build up more momentum before doing the second. Practice until you can do the board 360 quickly.

21 | Tail sink

Sail on a run or a very broad reach. Then step or jump back almost to the very end of the board. Be careful to place your weight squarely over the centerline, to avoid turning the board to one side or the other. Push up on the boom in such a way that you increase the downward force on the tail of the board, lifting the nose higher than would your weight alone. The stronger the wind, the nearer to vertical you can tilt the hull and still recover.

If you jump back when sailing fast in strong wind this becomes a flare. Instead of the tail immediately sinking, it skips along the surface, the nose pointing skyward.

Try sailing along in a tail sink, correcting the tendency to yaw from side to side by tilting the rig to one side or the other.

To bring the nose down, pull down on the boom to transfer your weight from the stern to the rig. If you are positioned correctly, it's possible to raise and lower the nose of the board by this means without moving your feet at all.

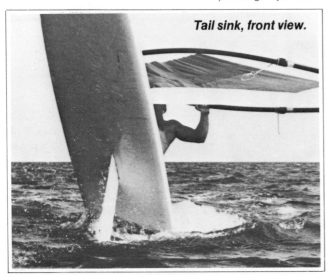

Tail sink, front view.

Tail sink, back view.

22 | Nose sink

A nose sink can be performed as a trick in itself or as a means of sailing stern first.

Sail normally and head up until the board points into the wind. Then quickly step onto the nose of the board, pulling the sail around with you, and sheet in for a stern-first run. You must be quick getting onto the nose, to lift the skeg clear of the water before it turns the stern into the wind.

Put very little force on the rig and keep your weight squarely over the centerline. Steer with the rig to stop the board turning to one side or the other.

... On one leg

Should an ordinary nose sink become too easy, try it one-footed. Place one foot in front of the other, both on the centerline, then slowly lift the forward foot from the water....

23 | Stern-first reach

It's possible to sail stern first for a short time without lifting the skeg clear of the water, if you continuously push the stern away from the wind with your feet. This is even possible on a reaching course.

While luffing, position the board on a beam reach. Hang part of your weight on the rig and place your feet between the daggerboard and the stern, on the extreme windward edge of the board. As you sheet in, push hard with your feet. Put most force on the foot nearest the wind.

The stronger the wind the harder it is to stop the stern from rounding up. When it does get the better of you, hang your weight on the rig and keep sheeting in, walking the hull around beneath you until it sails forward normally.

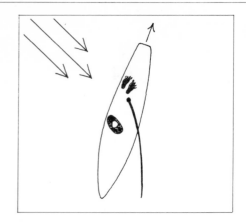

24 | Stern-first run

This method of sailing stern-first also uses the feet to push the stern off the wind.

To get into the position illustrated, sail normally, turn the board head-to-wind, then step aft a little and backwind the sail to sail downwind stern first.

Avoid putting weight too near the stern or you'll drive it underwater and immediately turn the board.

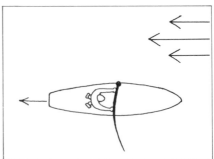

---

25 | Stern-first back-to-back

Doug Wilson sails stern-first toward us, his back to the lee side of the sail. Notice how he inclines the mast toward the stern and places his left foot between the end of the sailboard and the daggerboard to push the stern off the wind.

A stern-first back-to-back is primarily a light-wind maneuver, though it can be sustained for a short time in stronger wind.

Start by sailing forward on a close reach or beam reach. Luff, then turn around to face the stern, putting your back to the sail. Place one hand on the mast and reach along the boom with the other hand. Sheet in by pushing the clew toward the bow and, if necessary, leaning back into the sail.

As the board starts moving stern-first, the skeg will catch the water. Therefore, rake the mast to leeward and toward the stern, causing the stern to turn away from the wind. At the same time, push the stern away from the wind with a foot placed between the stern and the daggerboard. You may have to push very strongly. The nearer the wind the board turns, the harder it is to stop the stern from rounding into the wind. It's easiest on a beam reach or run.

A natural way out of the stern-first back-to-back position is to allow the stern to round up, walking the board around with your feet until you end up sailing forward (bow first) with your back to the lee side of the sail.

26 | Sail 360

For a sail 360, rotate the rig through 360° while you remain standing more or less in the same position. This isn't difficult to do smoothly once you've worked out the hand movements.

Before initiating the last half turn it's important you raise the mast fairly close to vertical, then pull the mast towards the wind as the clew flies to leeward, so the clew doesn't drag in the water.

1/Move your clew hand nearer the clew, selecting an underhand grip.

2/Transfer the mast hand to a position aft of the clew hand, and release the clew hand as the mast swings to leeward.

5/Keep the sail luffing in the clew-first orientation, and move your hands along the boom towards the mast as you lift the mast until it's almost vertical.

6/Put a hand on the mast, sheet in clew-first for a moment, then pull the mast strongly to windward as you let go with the clew hand, allowing the clew to fly to leeward.

3/Reach under the foot of the sail with the free hand, and grasp the other boom.

4/Quickly put both hands on the boom.

7/Change hands on the mast as the sail swings. Whether you hold the mast above or below the boom depends on personal preference.

8/Sheet in normally.

2/Grip the foot of the sail with your clew hand and pull the clew around into the eye of the wind, letting the mast swing to leeward over the stern.

3/Once the clew is in the eye of the wind, lift the rig to windward.

27 | Tack sail 360

In this variant of the sail 360 the hull is tacked but the sail 360 is started while the sail is still full on the original side. Though the illustration shows the 360 performed by holding the foot of the sail, it's possible to go directly from boom to boom.

Two common learning problems are hitting the water with the rig during the turn, and ending up with the sail full on the original tack. Be sure the hull has turned well onto the new tack before you start the sail 360. Then, hold the rig securely and pull it well to windward for each half-turn, so neither mast nor clew touches the water.

1/Tack, pulling the sail beyond the midline of the board to turn the hull well onto the new tack.

4/Let go of the foot of the sail and grab the mast, pulling it directly into the eye of the wind.

5/Pull the mast strongly to windward as you let the clew flip over the stern. If you don't, the booms will hit the water.

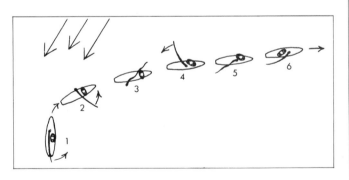

6/Having completed the sail 360, sheet in normally on the new tack and turn away from the wind.

28 | Ducktack

This doesn't mean to tack like a duck, but to duck under the sail as you tack.

The idea is to turn the board head-to-wind, throw the luffing sail directly into the wind, then quickly duck to the other side of the board, catch the boom, and turn away from the wind on the new tack. Speed and precision make this possible even in rough conditions.

In the photosequence I demonstrate the type of ducktack I personally favor.

Troubleshooting

□ At first you may reach the new side of the board only to find the sail filling on the original side. If you're already

1. Tilt the rig well aft and push with the rear foot to turn the board about 10° onto the new tack.

2. Luff the sail and tilt the mast forward, directly into the wind, letting the boom slide through your forward hand.

29 | Duckunder

A duckunder is similar to a ducktack, except that you don't tack the board.

Bring the board almost head-to-wind, throw the mast directly into the eye of the wind as for a ducktack, then duck under the sail and come up on the lee side. You can come up facing the sail or with your back to the sail.

Once on the lee side, lean the mast forward and push the bow off the wind with your forward foot.

In stronger wind, lean the mast to windward, closer to the water, before sheeting in. This reduces the sail's profile to the wind and reduces the chances of your being overpowered.

1. Bring the board almost head-to-wind, then tilt the rig forward into the eye of the wind.

sure that you are leaning the mast directly into the eye of the wind, the answer may be to tack more vigorously: as the board turns through the wind push away firmly with the rear foot and pull the sail over the board's midline. This should give the board sufficient momentum to keep it turning onto the new tack while you duck under the sail.

☐ With experience you'll find that position 2 (holding the luffing sail with one hand halfway back on the boom) still leaves you some control over the sail; even if it fills on one side or the other, it's possible to luff again.

☐ If the sail persists in filling on the original side just as you reach the new

side, you may still be able to recover by pulling it across the midline of the board and using your feet to push the board around onto the new tack.

Failing that, never say die, just turn the trick into something which calls for you to be facing the lee side of the sail.

3. When there's room to pass under the sail, stop the rig with one hand about midway along the boom. Then duck swiftly to the other side.

4. Pull the rig aft again, reaching for the new boom. Sheet in and bear off on the new tack.

2. Duck under the sail to the lee side of the board.

3. Put your back to the sail, lean the mast forward, and push the bow downwind with your forward foot.

30 | Duckspin tack

Add a spin to a ducktack and you have a duckspin tack. There are many ways of doing the trick, largely differences of rig control and of how and where the spin is performed. What's important is that you balance the rig well, spin swiftly, and ensure your timing is good.

In the photosequence, Gary Eversole balances the rig, then lets go and

1/Tack the board, tilting the rig well aft and pushing with the rear foot.

2/When the board is head-to-wind, throw the mast directly into the wind to the point where the rig balances; then let go and spin.

spins whilst still on the original side of the board.

An alternative is to do half the turn by stepping the forward foot back whilst holding the original boom above your head with your forward hand. Then, duck under the sail and pull the rig aft again, using the momentum of that pull to complete the spin on one foot.

3/Having completed the spin, step under the sail and pull the rig aft again.

4/Sheet in on the new tack and bear off.

31 | Clew power-through to clew-first

The clew power-through is a quick and effective way to maneuver the sail into clew-first orientation. Start by tacking the board and staying on the lee side of the sail as you turn away from the wind, then simply push the clew through the eye of the wind using the technique described in the photo-captions. It's fairly easy in wind under about 12 knots. When it becomes too easy, try it using only one hand.

Strong wind

In strong wind, before trying to power the clew through the wind, make the sail easier to handle by:
☐ bearing off to a broad reach to reduce apparent wind speed;
☐ leaning the mast to windward, nearer the water, while leaving the clew up.

1/ Tack, pulling the sail across the board to turn fully through the wind.

2/ Remain on the original side of the board as you fill the sail on the new tack, then steer away from the wind while facing the lee side of the sail. Steer at least 90° away from the wind before you attempt the clew power-through.

Tips on sailing clew-first

Up to now the term clew-first has been used without much explanation, so let's look at what it involves.

Clew-first means sailing with the clew nearest the wind, so that air enters the sail at the clew and leaves at the mast. Consequently the forward hand, though now the hand nearest the clew, performs all the functions it would if you were sailing normally. For example, it initiates steering movements and adjusts the angle at which the wind meets the sail. You now sheet in with the rear hand by pulling the mast toward you, and luff by pushing it away.

It's particularly important to hold the clew steady. If you don't, the entire rig will shake back and forth as the sail luffs and fills. You'll make the trick easier if you avoid pointing too near the wind.

One of the most graceful ways into clew-first sailing is to gybe the board without letting the clew flip over the bow, then head up clew-first on the new tack.

3/Position your hands on either side of the balance point of the boom, spacing them far enough apart to give the leverage necessary for the power-through. Now push hard with the clew hand, releasing pressure on the mast hand, so that the force of the wind in the sail pivots the rig around its balance point.

4/With the sail luffing clew-first, pull the mast toward yourself to sheet in.

1/Face the lee side of the sail and position the board at least 90° away from the wind.

2/Ease pressure off the mast hand and push hard with the clew hand. As the clew reaches the eye of the wind, release the boom with your mast hand, and spin beneath the clew arm.

32 | Clew power-through with skipper 360

To add a flourish to the clew power-through described in sequence 31, spin around under one arm as you push the clew into the eye of the wind. In the photographs, as the sail turns one way, Gary spins the opposite way.

33 | Spin gybe into clew-first sailing

A spin can be used to enhance many tricks. Here the skipper spins 360° while the board is gybed into clew-first orientation—a combination trick probably best reserved for light wind.

As described in sequence 32, the hand which holds the boom during your spin must turn over at some point. When it does, controlling the rig becomes a trick in itself. Though you can bend your wrist inside the boom for an instant as you roll the back of your hand over the boom, the rig will fall slightly to leeward, so follow it with your hand.

1/In light wind, gybe the board into clew-first sailing.

2/As you head up to a broad reach on the new tack, release with your mast hand and spin under your clew hand. The clew hand maintains contact with the boom throughout your spin.

3/Throughout most of your spin you can hold the boom with your clew hand, but at some time it must turn over. As it does, keep the rig balanced by rolling the back of your hand over the boom, knuckles inside.

4/Return both hands to the boom again and sheet in clew-first.

3/Return both hands to the boom as soon as possible, and sail clew-first.

34 Clew-first ducktack

A clew-first ducktack is difficult except in very light wind, and takes a lot of practice. Even in wind of just eight knots it's hard to get it right every time. The trick must be completed very quickly because the clew tends to spin one way or the other as you throw it into the eye of the wind.

1/Sail clew-first in light wind and tilt the rig far aft to tack the board.

2/As the board reaches head-to-wind, carefully throw the clew directly into the eye of the wind, then duck swiftly under or "behind" the mast, grabbing it with both hands.

3/When you reach the new side of the board, pull the mast aft again.

35 Clew-first duckunder

The clew-first duckunder puts you with your back to the lee side of a clew-first sail, so there are two aspects to this maneuver. The first is the duckunder, which is described in the photocaptions. The second is sailing back-to-back while clew-first, which is easier than you may think.

In fact it's possible to sail with your back to the lee side of a clew-first sail in fairly heavy wind. The harder it blows, the more you lean the rig aft and to windward, getting the sail down nearer the water. Use your body to sheet in and out. Luff in the gusts and, if necessary, push your body into the fabric to spill more air. There's a lot of pressure on your forward foot and you'll have to lean strongly back into the sail to maintain control.

Another way into the clew-first back-to-back position is with a fly-around, as illustrated in sequence 46.

4/Sheet in clew-first on the new tack.

36 | Clew-first inside the boom

Many tricks which are possible sailing normally can also be performed when the sail is in clew-first orientation, though sometimes with greater difficulty. A pirouette, ducktack and sailing inside the boom are examples of such tricks.

To sail clew-first inside the boom, simply sail clew-first, luff, then duck inside the boom and sheet in again.

In this position you can't counter gusts by leaning your body out over the water, so you'll have to luff, spilling excess air by letting the mast swing to leeward.

As a variation, try this with your body facing the other way, toward the wind.

1/Sail clew-first.

2/Luff. Lean the rig aft, grabbing the foot of the sail.

3/Duck to the other side of the sail, pulling it down behind your back.

4/Slip inside the boom as it descends. Push the mast to windward to sheet in clew-first with your back to the sail's lee side.

37 | Sail 180 with skipper 360

For a sail 180, spin the sail around 180°. You can start from clew-first orientation or from normal sailing, and spin the rig around in either direction.

In this sequence the sail starts from clew-first and the clew rotates to leeward while the skipper spins 360° in the opposite direction.

1/Sail clew-first.

2/Release the boom with the clew hand, letting the clew fly to leeward. As the sail spins one way, spin your body the other way, pulling the mast to windward and reaching around with your free hand to grasp the mast.

1/Sail clew-first, your clew hand holding the boom with an underhand grip.

2/Cross the mast hand over the clew hand, then duck inside the boom and simultaneously turn to face the wind without releasing the boom.

3/Lean the rig aft in order to head up and tack.

38 | Clew-first back-to-front, to clew-first back-to-back, then leeward walk

This is the most complex sequence so far, involving four main elements. In frame 1, the skipper sails clew-first. Between frames 1 and 2, he spins 180° to put himself inside the boom with his back to the windward side of

The board may turn toward the wind as you spin, bringing you uncomfortably close to the wind when you sheet in normally. You can avoid this by standing farther forward on the board and keeping the mast nearer upright, as for the spin gybe described earlier.

3/Holding the mast firmly in one hand, let go with the other hand and complete your spin.

4/Sheet in normally.

4/Tack the board without changing your position, thus putting your back to the lee side of the sail.

5/Remain inside the boom as you walk the rig around to leeward.

6/Sheet in facing the wind, inside the boom.

the sail. Frames 3 and 4 show him heading up and then tacking in clew-first orientation without changing his own position, thus putting his back to the lee side of the sail. Finally, in frames 5 and 6 he walks the rig

around to leeward into normal sail orientation and remains inside the boom facing the wind.

The photocaptions describe how this is accomplished.

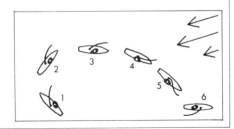

39 Sail 180 into back-to-back

A sail 180 provides an attractive, relatively easy way into a back-to-back (back to the lee side of the sail). I particularly like this method because it's swift and efficient, and doesn't leave you wobbling at the mercy of chop and gusts for long.

Sail clew-first, then release the clew so it flies over the bow, and, as you step around the mast, throw the rig behind your back, catching it with your forward hand.

To make the transition smoothly, leave your forward foot stationary in

1/Sail clew-first.

2/Release the boom with your clew hand, allowing the clew to fly to leeward, and pull the mast to windward to compensate for the force of the boom swinging away.

Tips on Sailing Back-to-Back

Sailing along in the back-to-back position is popular, perhaps because it's possible over a wide range of wind strength. You can even sail back-to-back while riding swells; this isn't very difficult, and is certainly exhilarating.

The following points will help overcome a few of the initial problems:
□ When you first get into the back-to-back position, it's often necessary to put one foot forward of the mast and push the bow downwind.
□ Once the board has turned sufficiently away from the wind you may wish to step aft to a more comfortable position. When you do move, be careful to let the boom slide across your back, and avoid taking the rig aft with you. The other danger is that you will inadvertently sheet in. To prevent this, it's a good idea to luff a little and tilt the mast slightly more to windward as you move.
□ Some people find it easier to sail inside the boom, holding the boom in front of themselves.

front of the mast the whole time and move by stepping the rear foot around the mast. In strong wind, when you release the clew, put plenty of muscle into pulling the mast to windward or else the momentum of the boom will pull you over the lee side. Once the clew is to leeward, don't stand around gingerly passing the rig from hand to hand behind your back while wind and chop buffet you. Quickly but precisely throw the rig into position behind your back, lean back and sheet in.

3/Leave the forward foot in place as you step the rear foot around the mast as smoothly and swiftly as you can, throwing the sail behind your back and catching the mast at hip height with your forward hand.

4/Sheet in, leaning the rig to windward and luffing if the wind is too strong.

Strong wind

☐ *If the wind is strong, then to avoid being overpowered, lean the mast to windward before you sheet in.*
☐ *The heavier the wind, the closer to the wind you may have to sail so that you can spill air in the gusts with very little body movement.*
☐ *Spilling air—luffing—takes a little practice; you have to twist your body whenever a gust hits.*
☐ *You can also make sail control easier if you push your body into the fabric. But be careful not to push the boom to windward or you'll put even more power in the sail.*

40 | Tack-and-turn into back-to-back

The tack-and-turn method of getting into a back-to-back lacks the flair of the sail 180 method, but is still classier than the basic 'stop sailing and step around the front of the mast' method.

Start out by sailing normally. Tack the board but remain standing on the lee side of the sail as you turn the board away from the wind on the new tack. Then, turn your back to the sail using the hand placement illustrated in frame 3.

There are two things to be especially careful of: first, that you luff

1/Tack the board, pulling the sail across the midline and pushing strongly with your rear foot in order to turn well through the wind.

2/Facing the lee side of the sail, turn the board away from the wind on the new tack. Keep the forward foot in front of the mast to give you the power to control the sail if gusts hit.

WIND

41 | Back-to-back, tack to back-to-front

Having mastered both a back-to-back and a back-to-front, you can link them together by turning the board back and forth onto alternate tacks while staying on the same side of the sail. Let's look at this frame by frame.

Frame 1 Sail with your back to the lee side of the sail. Then, tack the board by tilting the rig strongly aft and putting weight on the rear foot which you place aft of the daggerboard.

Frame 2 Keep the sail full on the original tack until the board has turned through the eye of the wind and well onto the new tack.

Frame 3 When the board is on the new tack, brace your forward foot against the mast step, then lean forward and fill the sail on the new tack too. Make all movements smoothly, so the board's momentum, which

before beginning to turn your body and, second, that when moving your feet you keep them on the midline of the board. Work out the foot placement and movement that suits you best.

3/Luff the sail while transferring the rear hand to the mast, thumb down. Step the rear foot forward of the mast, then step the forward foot aft.

4/Complete the turn by putting your hand aft on the boom.

carries it forward as you pass through the eye of the wind, is not disrupted. **Frame 4** Tilt the rig forward to turn away from the wind. Commit yourself to pulling strongly against the sail while being prepared to luff if it pulls you backward or makes you arch your shoulders backward. After some time on this tack, tack again so your back is once more against the lee side of the sail.

42 | Back-to-back clew power-through, then sail 180 with skipper 360

In this sequence, Gary sails with his back to the lee side of the sail, then powers the clew to windward into clew-first sailing. He holds clew-first sailing for a moment, then lets the clew blow around 180° to leeward while spinning himself the other way around, ending up in a normal sailing position.

Each of these moves has already been covered individually, but the way they're joined together here calls for several new techniques.

1/Sail back-to-back.

2/Slide the rig forward across your back until the mast swings off to leeward, causing the rig to pivot around your forward shoulder. This forces the clew to windward.

Notice how the rear hand is used to control the rig as the clew is **powered to windward. In frame 2, Gary's right hand is raised to the boom in an overhand grip, which enables him to retain hold as the rig flies into position 3. All he has to do is straighten his arm and slide his hand nearer the mast.**

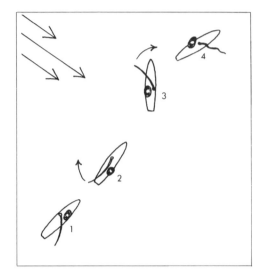

Troubleshooting

If the board turns into the wind as you spin, it may be because you step aft and lean the rig aft. Try moving your hands directly from boom to boom, eliminating the stage of holding the mast in one hand. See if this enables you to lean forward and counter the momentum of the rig without having to step aft. The method you use to control the rig as you spin depends on several factors, including your own style, physical flexibility and boom height. But, whatever your method, avoid leaning the rig aft.

3/Hold clew-first sailing for a moment, then let the clew fly over the bow.

4/As the sail spins 180°, spin your body in the opposite direction, leaning forward to counterbalance the rig, and either pass the mast from hand to hand or go directly from boom to boom. Having completed the spin, sheet in normally.

1/Gary sails stern-first toward shore.

2/His mast hand releases the boom, and he allows the mast to take its natural course as it swings to leeward.

43 | Flyaround

To do a flyaround, place the clew hand well on the clew side of the boom's balance point, then release the boom with the mast hand while holding on firmly with the clew hand. The mast will fly around to leeward, pivoting the rig around the clew hand and therefore forcing the clew to windward.

This is an attractive maneuver which can be used in many situations, a few of which are illustrated in this book. This particular sequence shows a flyaround being used to reverse direction from stern-first sailing to forward clew-first sailing.

Photosequence

Frame 1 Gary Eversole sails stern-first toward the shore. Preparing for the flyaround he has put his clew hand nearer the clew. **Frame 2** When he releases the boom with his mast hand, the mast swings to leeward. He leans back to counter its momentum and lets it take its natural course. The sail swings 180°, then stops and luffs, clew nearest the wind as in frame 3. **Frames 3-4** Gary steps aft and lifts the sail slightly to windward. **Frame 5** Sheeting in clew-first, he

sails away from the shore.

A flyaround isn't difficult in light and moderate wind, but in high wind the position of the clew hand becomes critical. If it's too near the boom's balance point the rig won't have sufficient momentum to power the clew to windward. If the clew hand is too near the clew, you may be pulled over forward or have the boom pulled out of your hand.

It isn't possible to prescribe a hand position that's correct for everyone. It depends on factors such as your arm length, boom height, and the sail you use.

3/Having pivoted 180°, the rig stops and luffs, clew nearest the wind.

4/Lifting the rig to windward, Gary prepares to sheet in clew first.

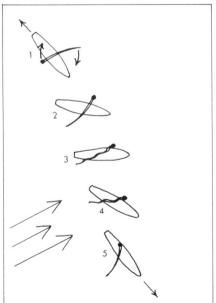

5/He sails forward, clew-first.

1/Sail with your back to the windward side of the sail and position your clew hand well aft of the boom's balance point.

2/Release the mast, allowing it to swing to leeward.

4/Reach under the foot of the sail and grasp the other boom.

5/While luffing the sail, clew nearest the wind, lift the rig to windward and get both hands onto the boom.

44 Back-to-front duckunder flyaround

If you initiate a flyaround when doing a back-to-front hang-out (hanging outside the boom with your back to the windward side of the sail), you have several interesting possibilities. One is the duckunder flyaround.

As you release the mast with the forward hand, simultaneously turn to meet the clew, which will pivot toward you. Then, duck under the sail, turn toward the bow, and sheet in clew first.

This maneuver is difficult in heavy wind, because the mast swings off

with a lot of momentum. In that case, be sure your clew hand is the correct distance aft of the boom's balance point before letting the mast go.

If you don't duck under the foot of the sail as it swings around into the clew-first orientation, but instead remain on the same side of the fabric and step forward with the sail, you can end up facing the lee side of a clew-first sail. This position is illustrated in trick 45.

3/While the rig spins one way, turn your body the opposite way, retaining hold of the boom with your clew hand.

Facing the lee side of a clew-first sail.

6/Pull the mast toward you to sheet in clew-first.

45 | Facing the lee side of a clew-first sail

A flyaround also provides an effective way of getting yourself facing the lee side of a clew-first sail. You can do the flyaround from normal sailing, or from the back-to-front hang-out position illustrated in frame 1 of sequence 44.

The back-to-front hang-out can be done with the forward hand on the mast or on the boom. Either way, move the clew hand aft along the boom, then let go with the forward hand and retain hold with the clew hand, allowing the mast to swing 180° to leeward (a flyaround). As the clew spins toward you, step around the front of the mast. Luff clew-first and face the sail as you raise it toward the wind. Get both hands onto the boom again, and push the mast away from you to sheet in clew-first, facing the lee side of the sail.

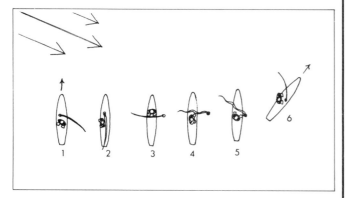

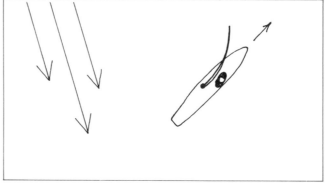

1/Sail on a beam reach. Step your forward foot just forward of the mast and, using an underhand grip, shift your clew hand slightly aft.

2/Release the boom with your mast hand.

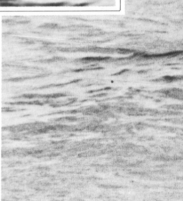

46 | Flyaround into clew-first back-to-back

The maneuver illustrated here, a flyaround into the clew-first back-to-back position, can be performed even in fairly strong wind.

Spin the rig 180° using the usual flyaround technique: releasing with the mast hand and retaining hold of the boom with the clew hand. As the clew pivots toward you, guide the sail into position behind your back. Luff clew-first as you lift the rig slightly to windward and slip inside the boom, then sheet in clew-first by pushing the mast to windward.

Roger Jones demonstrates.

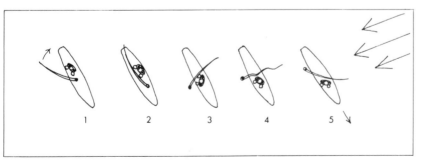

3/Hold the rig with a straight arm as the mast swings away, leaning back to counter its momentum.

4/When the clew reaches the eye of the wind, keep the sail luffing as you lift the rig to windward, slip inside the boom, and get both hands on the boom.

5/Sheet in clew-first, with your back to the lee side of the sail. In strong wind, don't sheet in until you've leaned the mast well aft and to windward or you'll be overpowered. Initially, you may have to move your forward foot to leeward and bend your knees, to push back really hard against the sail and stop yourself being blown face down.

47 | Sail & skipper leeward walk

This method of returning to normal sailing from the clew-first back-to-back position was illustrated in sequence 38, as part of a combination.

Simply stay inside the boom as you walk the rig around to leeward. Either sheet in facing the wind inside the boom, or duck out and sheet in normally.

This is easy in light wind. In heavy wind it's more difficult, and a sail 180 is a safer means of returning to normal sailing. The sail 180 can be done by spinning the rig either in a clew-to-windward direction or a clew-to-leeward direction.

48 | Luff & steparound

Another way out of a clew-first back-to-back is to luff the sail clew-first, then step around the mast and let the

1/Roger Jones sails clew-first, his back to the lee side of the sail.

2/He walks the rig around to leeward . . .

1/Sail clew-first back-to-back.

3/. . . sheeting in, inside the boom with his back to the windward side of the sail.

4/Sheet in clew-first on the windward side.

clew fly to leeward into normal
orientation.
    Alternatively, you could luff clew-
first then duck under the foot of the
sail to the windward side.

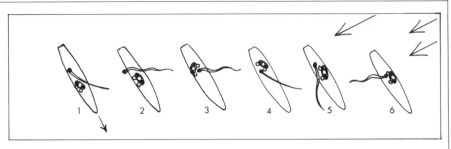

2/Luff clew-first.

3/Step around the mast.

5/Allow the clew to swing to leeward.

6/Sheet in normally.

49 | Helicopter

In a helicopter, sometimes called a sail 360, skipper and sail rotate together through 360°. This trick was popularized by Mark Robinson of Florida, whose powerful performances in wind over 25 knots drew enthusiastic applause from audiences in international freestyle championships.

By alternately exerting and relieving pressure on either side of the boom's balance point, you can make the force of the wind rotate the rig for you. Remember, the stronger the wind the more you incline the rig to windward at the beginning, to cut just as large a slice of wind as you can handle.

Troubleshooting

☐ If the sail, instead of flying around, collapses onto the water somewhere between positions 3 and 4, you probably leaned the mast too near the water and at the same time failed to properly backwind the sail.
☐ A good understanding of the balance point of the boom is essential. You must also know where the mast and boom will swing at various stages of the helicopter, so you're neither knocked off backward by the mast blowing to leeward nor, later on, dragged off forward by the clew blowing to leeward.
☐ To be graceful, concentrate on good footwork, and stay near the mast so you can pivot around it.

1/Sail on a beam reach.

4/As the rig pivots around its balance point, step around after it.

2/Swing the clew to leeward to luff the sail while dipping the mast to windward as much as wind strength demands.

3/Step forward of the mast and backwind the sail. Keep your body clear of the mast as you push hard on the boom with the clew hand and release some pressure on the mast hand to let the mast blow to leeward.

5/When the clew passes through the wind, the sail fills on your side and wants to complete its turn quickly. Therefore, pull the mast toward you while allowing the clew to swing over the stern, pivoting your body around after it as gracefully as you can.

6/At the end of the spin the sail may pull hard, so be ready to control it by extending your arms and, if necessary, dropping your weight low.

50 | Reverse helicopter

1/Sail on a beam reach and place your clew hand well aft on the boom.

2/Release the boom with your mast hand, leaning back to counter the force of the mast swinging away.

3/The rig pivots around your clew hand, forcing the clew to windward. As the rig spins, let it take its own path at its own speed. When it slows, step around after it.

4/As the clew reaches the eye of the wind, return both hands to the boom and backfill the sail. Push the mast to windward, allowing the clew to fly over the bow at its own speed.

5/Step around rapidly to keep up with the rig.

A reverse helicopter rotates the opposite way from a standard helicopter, starting with the mast swinging to leeward and the clew swinging to windward. It can be performed either by releasing the boom with the mast hand at the beginning, or by keeping both hands on the boom the entire time.

In this photosequence, the reverse helicopter is performed by letting go with the mast hand. Think of the maneuver as being in two parts. The first part (frames 1-4) is a flyaround: let go with your mast hand and hold the boom with the clew hand. Lean back to counter the force of the mast swinging away, and step around with the rig as you let it follow its natural path.

In the second part of the maneuver, backfill the sail clew-first, and step close to the mast. From this relatively safe position, push the mast to windward while allowing the clew to spin to leeward at its own speed.

6/Fill the sail normally.

51 | Nosewalk reverse helicopter

When a reverse helicopter is started in the nosewalk position it looks and feels different from the standard reverse helicopter. The nosewalk reverse helicopter can be done in wind ranging from eight knots to 20 knots or more, depending on your ability, strength, weight and the size of your sail. It should be started on a broad reach.

Frames 1-3: the nosewalk

The nosewalk can be performed without the helicopter. Start by placing your forward hand on the mast below the boom. Bend at the knees to bring your body near the board. Then hang your weight entirely on the rig as you walk your feet onto the nose of the board, leaving your torso aft of the mast.

Hold the nosewalk for a few moments. Ideally, your legs will be straight, as far onto the nose of the board as you can put them and still remain in control. Your body will be in a graceful arc.

Frames 4-7: the reverse helicopter

The nosewalk position and the hand on the mast enable you to stay close to the mast and pivot your body around it during the reverse helicopter. This is important, because once you start there isn't time to move any dis-

tance across the board. Everything happens very fast, and if you aren't able to let the rig continue all the way around at its own speed it'll probably flatten you.

By starting the nosewalk reverse helicopter while sailing away from the wind—on a broad reach, for example—you reduce apparent wind velocity, making the trick easier. Try it also while riding swells. At times this can reduce apparent wind so much that the rig feels almost weightless. Following is a frame-by-frame

1/Sail on a broad reach. Hold the mast with your forward hand below the boom, and drop your body near the board.

4/Keep your body close to the mast and initiate the reverse helicopter by pulling the clew into the wind in one quick motion.

5/Pivot your body around the mast as the rig turns, and when the clew enters the eye of the wind, stand up. As the sail backfills, push the mast to windward and down toward the water while letting the clew blow around to leeward.

account of the reverse helicopter section of the sequence.

Frame 4 In the nosewalk position, draw your legs in nearer the mast, as shown. Then, initiate the reverse helicopter by oversheeting the sail, pulling the clew into the wind in one quick motion, and letting the mast swing very slightly to leeward at the same time.

Frame 5 When the clew enters the eye of the wind, the rig suddenly feels as if it's in neutral, neither pushing nor pull-ing. While the sail luffs clew-first, quickly stand up and step around the mast, pivoting on the foot nearest the mast, ready to push hard against the mast the moment the sail backfills. **Frame 6** As the sail backfills, push the mast aft and to windward, inclining it toward the water. Pivot your body around the mast very quickly as your clew hand flops the sail up and around to leeward.

Frame 7 Sheet in normally.

2/Hanging your weight on the rig, walk your legs onto the nose leaving your torso aft of the mast.

3/Hold the nosewalk position for a moment.

6/With the mast near the water, the rapid movement of the clew blowing to leeward becomes easier to handle, provided you push hard on the mast and pivot your body very swiftly on the foot nearest the mast.

7/Pull your clew hand around rapidly after your body and fill the sail normally.

73

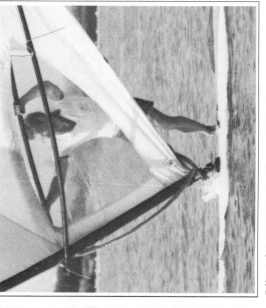

9/While the sail spins and fills on the other side, use your mast hand to throw the mast toward the bow and to windward to a position where it will balance long enough for you to spin 360°

10/Spin swiftly.

5/Let the mast swing toward the bow as you push hard with the clew hand, pivoting the rig around its balance point. When you push the clew through the eye of the wind, the sail fills clew-first, as shown in frame 6.

6/Compare mast and clew positions in frames 4, 5 and 6: to pivot the rig around its balance point, you must push the clew to windward the same degree and at the same time as the mast swings to leeward.

Frames 1-6: clew-first reverse helicopter

1/Sail clew-first on a beam reach.

2/Release the boom with your clew hand, allowing the clew to fly to leeward at its own speed as you pull the mast to windward with a straight arm.

74

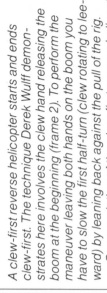

11/ Grab the boom and sheet in normally.

Frames 7-11: sail 180 with skipper 360

7/ With the sail full in clew-first orientation, release with the clew hand.

52 | Clew-first reverse helicopter, then sail 180 with skipper 360

A clew-first reverse helicopter starts and ends clew-first. The technique Derek Wulff demonstrates here involves the clew hand releasing the boom at the beginning (frame 2). To perform the maneuver leaving both hands on the boom you have to slow the first half-turn (clew rotating to leeward) by leaning back against the pull of the rig.

On completion of the clew-first reverse helicopter, Derek again lets go with his clew hand, allowing the sail to spin 180° while he spins 360° in the opposite direction, to end up sailing normally. Instead of passing the mast from hand to hand the way Gary Eversole does for the same move in sequence 37, Derek throws the rig toward the wind and toward the bow, balancing it so he can release with both hands and spin.

Whether you release the rig with both hands or pass the mast from hand to hand as you spin, avoid stepping aft or leaning the mast aft, otherwise the board will turn toward the wind.

8/ As the clew swings to leeward, pull the mast to windward with a straight arm and use the free arm to initiate body rotation—notice in frames 8, 9 and 10 the free arm thrown in the direction of rotation.

3/ The sail slows as it approaches the wind. Step and pivot your body swiftly to catch up with it.

4/ Place both hands on the boom, one either side of the balance point, and backwind the sail.

Frames 7-9;
sail 180

7

4

8

5

Frames 1-3: tack to finish
facing the lee side of
the sail, then
clew power-through

1

2

9

6

*Frames 3–7:
clew-first reverse helicopter*

3

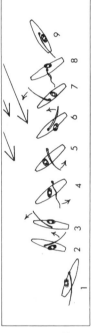

9

8

7

6

5

4

3

2

1

53 | Tack, clew power-through, clew-first reverse helicopter, then sail 180 (egg-beater)

In this four-move combination the sail spins continuously through two full revolutions, hence the name egg-beater. Gary starts the sequence by tacking without crossing to the other side of the sail. Then, facing the lee side of the sail, he turns the hull away from the wind. When it's about 45° from the wind he performs a clew power-through, followed without pause by a clew-first helicopter and sail 180.

1/Tack without moving to the other side of the sail, then turn the board at least 45° away from the wind while you face the lee side of the sail.

2/Lean the mast toward the wind and relax pressure on the mast hand as you push hard with the clew hand to power the clew through the eye of the wind into clew-first orientation.

3/When the sail fills clew-first, release the boom with your clew hand. As you let the clew blow across the bow at its own speed, pull the mast to windward with the mast hand, keeping the mast arm extended.

4/As the sail slows, step around after it. Return both hands to the boom and lean the mast toward the wind. In strong wind lean the mast well to windward.

5/This is the first stage of a clew power-through. Backwind the sail and, with the mast leaning toward the water, let the mast swing forward as you push hard with the clew hand.

6/Compare sail positions in frames 5 and 6 to see how Gary pivots the rig around its balance point. As he pushed the clew to windward he allowed the mast to swing an equal degree to leeward.

7/Between frames 6 and 7, Gary lets the mast swing to leeward slightly while pushing hard with his clew hand, causing the rig to pivot sufficiently to power the clew through the eye of the wind. When the sail fills clew-first, release the boom with the clew hand, letting the sail swing to leeward.

8/As the sail swings, avoid stepping aft or leaning the rig aft, as these actions will turn the board toward the wind.

9/Catch the boom and sheet in normally.

4/As you come out of the water, sheet out a little to stop yourself being launched into the air.

3/If necessary, drop one hand onto the mast below the boom. Sheet out a fraction, then, as the board speeds up, sheet in again and the sail will lift you. The rear hand controls sheeting while the forward hand does most of the lifting.

2/Set the board on a beam reach by positioning both feet well aft on the hull while you lean the sail forward. This way your feet can push the bow nearer the wind to counter the effect of the sail turning it away from the wind.

1/Hold the sail overhead, mast perpendicular to the wind. Lean the sail forward to keep the board from turning into the wind, and get your forward foot on the board as soon as possible.

The water start is a useful trick which saves time and energy getting up after a fall. Though fairly difficult it's worth mastering, especially for sailing in surf.

The best way to practice is to repeatedly lower yourself slowly into the water while you're sailing, then lift yourself out again. You'll need at least 12 knots of wind, and water shallow enough to stand on the bottom if necessary.

Lowering yourself into the water

Even lowering yourself into the water has to be done carefully if you aren't to be dragged off the board.

First, head up to slow down, then sheet out to let yourself gradually into the water. Once body resistance has slowed the board considerably, bear off slightly to increase lift in the sail so you continue to sink in a controlled fashion. Keep some wind in the sail and keep your heels on the board.

Raising the mast from the water

If the sail is lying in the water after a fall, grab the mast with both hands and lift it overhead. Be prepared to go right to the mast tip if necessary.

Lift the mast as high as possible, maneuvering it until it's perpendicular to the wind. As the wind gets under the sail, walk your hands down the mast and get your rear hand onto the boom.

Pull the boom toward the water while you hold the mast up and move it slightly toward the wind. This keeps the sail full. You must incline the rig toward the bow or the board will turn into the wind and cause the sail to collapse on you again. Steer with the sail as you would normally.

Get your forward foot onto the board as soon as possible, then the other foot.

Using your legs

Once your feet are on the board use them to push and pull the board onto a beam reach. Keeping a beam reach heading requires continuous maneuvering, which can be aided by positioning both feet well aft. Then when you lean the rig forward the bow turns off the wind, and when you push the stern away with your feet you turn the bow toward the wind.

Takeoff

With the sail full overhead and the board on a beam reach, lift yourself out of the water as shown.

Light air

A water start is possible even in very light wind if you put your forward hand low on the mast, hold the foot of the sail, and let the wind lift the rig until it's vertical before putting your weight on it. Once your feet are on the board, pull your chest in close to your knees to get as near the hull as possible. Then pull vertically down through the rig to pull yourself into a crouching position on the board.

1

2

6

5

4

3

55 | Backflip into water start

A wind speed of about 12 knots is ideal for this trick.

Sail on a reach. Lean the mast to windward. Bend your knees. Then, spring up, passing your legs between the sail and the boom. Put all your weight onto the boom to lift yourself through, and complete the somersault into the water.

It's important that you lean the mast to windward and, even as you jump up, keep a steady downward force on the boom. Otherwise, the rig will blow off to leeward and you'll end up lying on top of it on the wrong side of the board.

In a 12-knot wind you won't have much trouble keeping the sail full above you, so you can water start to lift yourself out of the water.

It's possible to do a backflip and land on the board, but much more difficult, requiring precise judgement of how much to tilt the rig to windward and how much weight to put on the boom as you pass through.

The frontflip dismount could be used at the end of a competitive freestyle routine, or anytime you feel like cooling off in style. It's relatively easy, a fitting end to this section of body and sail tricks.

All you do is somersault forward over the boom. Keep hold of the boom and, as the rig falls into the water, simply land flat on your back on the sail, inside the boom.

You wouldn't want to do this with a prized racing sail, but if you fall flat on the sail and avoid putting your foot through the window, the trick won't do your everyday play sail any more harm than many of the other things you do with it.

56 | Frontflip dismount

57 | Windward railride

Riding the rail is one of the most popular freestyle moves. It isn't very difficult if you use the technique described in the following paragraphs. When practicing, bear in mind that lifting the rail and balancing are both easier in wind of eight to 15 knots than in lighter wind. Derek Wulff demonstrates.

Frame 1 Sail on a beam reach and load part of your weight onto the boom, making sure you don't lean the rig aft. Some people find that using an underhand grip on the boom enables them to support their weight better.

Place the rear foot to leeward, just aft of the daggerboard well, and push the lee rail down. Meanwhile, lift the windward rail by hooking the forward foot under it.

Frame 2 As the windward rail comes up, transfer most of your weight onto the boom and use your feet to continue pivoting the hull around its centerline.

Frame 3 The board pops up the last few degrees easily, because your weight exerts leverage through the mast foot (which, remember, pivots a few inches off the deck). When the rail reaches vertical, put your weight entirely on the boom while you lift the rear foot onto the rail and slide the forward foot down onto the daggerboard immediately beside the well. Luff or sheet in as necessary to balance.

Frame 4 Putting your foot on the daggerboard at the well stabilizes the railride for several reasons: (1) When a sailboard is on the rail it pivots around an axis running approximately through the daggerboard well, and keeping most of your weight on this axis removes a lot of leverage from the rail. (2) If necessary you can counterbalance the hull by levering it in opposite directions with either foot; however, avoid using so much force that you damage the daggerboard or the well. (3) The forward foot on the daggerboard enables you to press the side of your leg against the bottom of the hull for more stability.

As you gain experience, try to eliminate one foot on the daggerboard, and put both feet directly onto the rail as soon as it reaches vertical.

Frame 5 When you feel ready, lift the forward foot onto the rail. Balance is more critical now. You'll have to rely on shifting your weight and sheeting in and out to correct the slightest tilting of the hull. You can also use the mast against the rail to some extent.

Keep glancing down at the rail. If it tilts to windward, sheet in to pull it back up immediately.

If the rail leans to leeward, sheet out, because the sail is pulling you over. With experience, you'll also be able to correct a leeward list by pulling the mast to windward slightly as you sheet out, thus levering the rail to windward. Should the board tilt a long way to leeward before you can correct it, let it go all the way over unless you're very experienced, or you may break something.

Preparing your equipment

Before rushing out to try a railride, your equipment will need some attention.

It's important that the universal is firmly fixed into the sailboard so that it doesn't come out when you lean the rail against the mast.

Railriding can put high stress on the mast, at the bot-

tom end and where the boom attaches. Prevention is easier than cure, so I recommend reinforcing a freestyle mast with fiberglass tape and epoxy resin. You'll find the technique in chapter 8 (Maintenance) of my book Windsurfing with Ken Winner. Of course, one disadvantage of reinforcing is a heavier mast.

Troubleshooting

□ **Turning toward the wind:** If you perform a forward windward railride at 90° to the wind, you should be able to hold a steady course. However, if you start higher than 90° to the wind, the sailboard's configuration will make it turn toward the wind. You can stop the board turning upwind by putting more weight on the stern, causing the bow to lift. When the bow lifts, the board's center of lateral resistance shifts aft, which has the same effect as moving the sail's center of effort forward.

By sinking the tail sufficiently, you can make the sailboard turn downwind. Conversely, by sinking the nose you can make the board head up.

□ **Overbalancing as the rail pops up:** Sometimes the board pops onto the rail with such momentum that it continues all the way over. To prevent this, luff as it reaches vertical, then sheet in again when you've caught your balance.

□ **Failure to hold your weight on the rig:** Be sure to put your weight on the boom as the rail comes up, or you'll slide down and land with your rear thigh over the rail. Some people intentionally slump down like this before putting their forward foot onto the daggerboard. Though they probably believe this makes things easier, it looks clumsy and creates additional balance problems when they try to stand up again.

□ **Excessive effort to raise the rail:** Think of yourself as pivoting the hull around its midline, rather than 'lifting' the rail. Beginners are often seen straining to raise the rail, yet it comes up without much physical effort if you hang your weight on the boom at the beginning.

There are several reasons why hanging your weight on the boom helps. One is that your weight cannot accidentally encumber the rails, and so wind and water can exert their maximum turning effects. Traveling through the water the daggerboard tends to lift the windward rail slightly. In addition, the sailboard drifts slightly to leeward because of the sideways component of the sail's driving force. Consequently, as you push the lee rail underwater, it grabs and tends to be forced down and around to windward.

I've already mentioned the additional leverage of your weight acting down on the mast foot, which helps the board pop up the last few degrees to meet the mast.

When you're out in high wind using a full daggerboard, these forces can lift the board onto the rail with little or no help from you. Sometimes all you need do is hang most of your weight on the boom and the rail pops up.

This account of causes is provisional, because the dynamics of freestyle are complex and there may be forces I've not considered.

□ **Difficulty lowering the hull:** As if balancing isn't problem enough, it can also be difficult to get the hull down when you want to. You may have to sheet out and determinedly lever the windward rail down.

1/Sail on a beam reach. Hook your forward foot under the windward rail, and push the lee rail down with the other foot.
2/As the windward rail rises, put most of your weight on the boom and use your feet to pivot the hull about its centerline.
3/When the rail pops up, hang all your weight on the boom, lift the rear foot onto the rail, and slide the forward foot down to the daggerboard.
4/With the forward foot on the daggerboard beside the well, press the side of your forward leg against the bottom of the board for greater stability. Sheet in and out for balance.
5/Balance is more critical with both feet on the rail. Correct the slightest tilt immediately.

58 Righting the board... without getting wet

If you find yourself squatting on a board which turned turtle while you were trying to ride the rail, there are several ways to right it without getting into the water. Use the method shown in the photos only if the entire rig is reliably held together.

A safer though less showy method, not shown here, is to kneel on the upside down board, hook one leg under one rail, heel pressing on the deck, and push down on the opposite rail with the other shin and foot to lever the board over.

As the rail comes up, get one hand on the mast and the other on the upper rail, transfer your weight to your hands, then let the board roll beneath you—easier to do than to describe!

1/Grab the uphaul and put a foot on either rail. Pull the mast out of the water and lever the rail up with it. Hook a foot over the rising rail and help it up while the other foot pushes the opposite rail down.

59 Stern-first windward railride

To do a stern-first railride, you must get the board onto the rail the moment you sheet in, otherwise the stern will turn toward the wind. Fortunately, the rail pops up easily for a stern-first windward railride.

Though the board turns into the wind until the rail is up, once on the rail it turns away from the wind until you move your feet forward of the mast (the forward end being the stern in this case). Balance becomes increasingly difficult once a railride has turned more than 90° from the wind, so the best compromise is to start between a close reach and a beam reach.

The technique

I find the easiest way into the starting position shown in frame 1 is to sail normally, then lean the mast aft and head up until head-to-wind. Instead of tacking, keep the sail full and pull it around with you as you step forward of the mast to the other side of the board. You'll have to be quick getting your foot under the new windward rail, and lift the board when it's on just the heading you want.

Another way into the starting position is to stop sailing and, luffing the sail so as not to move in either direction, maneuver the board until the stern points between a close reach and a beam reach. Before sheeting in, place the forward foot under the windward rail. Lift it the moment you sheet in, simultaneously pushing the lee rail down with the rear foot.

Once again, whichever method you use to get the board on the desired heading prior to lifting the rail, the rail pops up most readily if you hang most of your weight on the rig and use your feet to pivot the hull.

As the rail comes up, you'll probably find it easiest to hold your weight on the boom as you drop the forward foot onto the daggerboard at the well, and then lift the rear foot onto the rail. When you feel ready, lift the for-

2/When the board is vertical put all your weight on the upper rail and turn the board entirely over.

3/Hop onto the deck as the board flops down.

ward foot onto the rail. As your technique improves, learn to put your forward foot directly onto the rail without using the daggerboard.

Steering the railride

The first problem is to stop the board from turning downwind. The easiest way is by walking forward of the mast to sink the stern slightly. As you walk forward, sheet out a little to slow the board and avoid being pulled over.

There are at least two reasons why walking forward stops the board turning downwind. By lifting the scooped nose you reduce its steering effect. You also shift the hull's center of lateral resistance forward, which has the same effect as moving the sail's center of effort aft in normal sailing.

The board also heads up if you lean the rail to windward, probably because this allows the nose to slice through the water and slide sideways.

To turn the board downwind, all you need do is remain standing on the rail above the mast step. To turn more quickly, walk aft to sink the nose slightly.

If your feet slip, consider roughening the rails. Some people use coarse sandpaper or a woodrasp; I use a fine-toothed saw dragged sideways.

60 | Stern-first railride with bodyhang sternwalk

In trick 59 I described how to stop a stern-first railride turning downwind by walking toward the stern. You can stand upright and walk your entire body sternward, or do a bodyhang sternwalk as shown here—keep the rig vertical and hang your weight on it; then, with very little weight on your feet, walk or shuffle along the rail toward the stern. You'll find the main problem is the board turning downwind before you can get your feet near enough to the stern to establish a steady course.

It's possible to do a bodyhang sternwalk in wind as light as five knots, since you hang your weight downward on the rig and don't rely on the wind to hold you.

1

61 | Nose sink on a stern-first railride

For this trick you must sink the nose before the board turns downwind. Position yourself about a meter from the nose. Push down with the rear foot and, as the nose sinks, pull the mast back toward you.

In this situation, the sail's center of effort is aft of the hull's center of resistance, as you can see by examining the photograph. This pivots the hull toward the wind. You can't do a deep nose sink for long because the board will turn too near the wind.

Before the board turns too close to the wind, step forward and lower the stern to the water. Continue sailing on the rail normally until the board bears off slightly, then push down with the rear foot to sink the nose again. Watch you don't put your weight so close to the end of the board that it rises to vertical; if you slip off, the board will jump out of the water and you'll find yourself dodging sharp edges.

62 | Nose sink on a forward railride

Walk along the rail toward the bow, sheeting out as much as necessary to remain balanced. Once you get to the nose, press your weight down and sink it. While in the nose sink you'll have to sheet in and out constantly to maintain balance and avoid being overpowered.

A nose sink causes the railride to turn toward the wind, so that by frame 4 the board is head-to-wind. From this position you have the choice of letting the board roll either way. You could drop it down right side up and sail out stern first as in sequence 83. Or you could roll the board all the way over, pull the clew around to windward, and head up for a stern-first everoll, as in sequence 82.

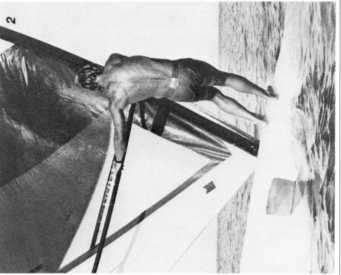

63 | Tack on the rail

A tack on the rail involves tacking the board and sail while the skipper remains on the original side of the sail, which has become the lee side.

Once you're proficient at railriding this won't be difficult. Moderate wind makes it easier than light wind, because, when you backwind the sail and lean forward, there's less likelihood of going down into the water. It's also easier with your forward foot on the daggerboard than with both feet on the rail.

One problem you may encounter is that though you successfully backwind the sail, you can't turn the board away from the wind, and find yourself balanced on the rail with the board stalled. To avoid this, make sure you turn the board well through the eye of the wind by over-sheeting as shown in frame 2. Then, having backwinded the sail, encourage the board to turn away from the wind by weighting your aft foot to sink the tail slightly and lift the nose. If you still fail to turn away from the wind and the board begins rolling upside down, let it roll and go into a stern-first everoll, as shown in sequence 86.

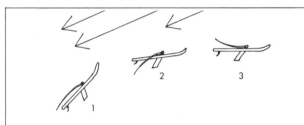

1/Head up on a forward windward railride by sinking the nose of the board slightly to shift the board's center of lateral resistance forward. Your forward foot should be forward of the mast, the rear foot just behind the mast and either on the rail or on the daggerboard.

64 | Back-to-front on the rail

By back-to-front I mean with your back to the windward side of the sail. One way into this position is to do a normal windward railride and then turn around. Gary Eversole recommends starting close-hauled on the rail, so you can reach the boom without difficulty when you turn around.

Before turning, luff a bit so as not to be pulled over. Then, slide the rear hand along the boom nearer the mast. Release the boom with your forward hand and step around, turning your back to the sail and reaching aft to grab the boom again. Here, Gary is completing his turn by reaching back to grab the boom with his right hand.

2/When the board is head-to-wind, oversheet the sail, pulling it over the hull; this causes the board to turn through the eye of the wind onto the new tack.

3/Once on the new tack, push the sail away from you to fill it on the other side, and lean it forward to turn away from the wind.

65 | Clew-first railride with one foot on the mast

Sail clew-first on the rail with the forward foot placed on the daggerboard beside the daggerboard well. Lift your rear foot up to the mast, then hang your body out as far from the mast as you can, hanging your weight vertically down on the boom so it is transmitted through the rig to the mast step.

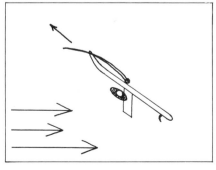

66 | Back-to-back stern-first railride

Back-to-back railrides can be performed by using a half-raised daggerboard to lever the rail up, or by using a foot on each rail. This version uses the daggerboard, which puts a lot of stress on the equipment.

1/Sail on a beam reach, luff the sail completely, and raise the daggerboard partway. Turn to face the stern with your back to the sail. If you slip inside the boom you'll find it easier to put most of your weight on the boom for the next stage.

2/You must get the rail up before the stern rounds into the wind. Therefore, as you sheet in to sail stern first, take most of your weight on the boom, push the lee rail down with the rear foot, and use the forward foot against the side of the daggerboard to lever the windward rail up. Don't sheet in too much or you'll be pushed over.

3/Lift the rear foot onto the rail as soon as you can.

4/Keep the board on the rail by counterbalancing the pressure of the forward foot on the dagger-board with that of the rear foot on the rail and, if necessary, by leaning the mast against the rail.

67 | Back-to-back railride sailing forward

This style of back-to-back railride puts less strain on equipment than using the daggerboard for leverage.

Though for a standard forward railride it's best to start on a beam reach, it's probably better to start this trick on a close reach. Any farther off the wind and the sail will be too far away from the board for you to stand on the rail. Depending on the cut of your sail, you may have trouble finding room for your feet between rail and sail.

1/Sail on a close reach with your back to the lee side of the sail. Duck inside the boom, and load most of your weight onto the boom in front of you.

68 | Stationary railride

The idea here is to hold the board stationary on the rail, the hull aligned with the wind, or only a few degrees off at most, so you can luff or fill the sail on either side with only a small movement.

The starting position is facing the lee side of the sail, with the board flat on the water at about 45° to the wind. Lean the mast toward the wind a

1/Face the lee side of the sail with the board at 45° to the wind. Lean the mast slightly to windward and push the lee rail down with the rear foot. Hook the arch of your forward foot over the windward rail as it rises, and lift the rail to touch the mast.

2/With the board more or less aligned with the wind, luff the sail so the board doesn't progress through the water. Balance unaided by the wind as far as possible.

2/Push the lee rail down with the rear foot, then hook the forward foot under the windward rail and lift it.

3/When the rail is vertical, hook the arch of your rear foot over it to hold it up while you lift the forward foot onto the rail.

little as you push the lee rail down with the rear foot (see frame 1). Hook the arch of your forward foot over the windward rail as it rises, and lift the rail to touch the mast.

Once on the rail, the board will turn into the wind. Hold the hull vertical, threequarters of your weight on the foot resting on the rail, the remainder hanging vertically down on the rig. Press the rear leg against the deck for extra stability. Now, luff the sail, and balance on the rail unaided by the wind. This is the situation in frame 2.

Keep looking down to check that the board is vertical; correct it the moment it tilts one way or the other. If you start falling backward, catch yourself by filling the sail on your side. If you fall forward, push away from yourself and backwind the sail.

In heavy wind it's difficult to stop the board traveling through the water.

4/Stand as soon as possible, and maintain contact between the rail and mast. Luff if the wind pushes you to leeward; sheet in if the board falls to windward.

1/Perform a clew-first windward railride and stabilize yourself on the rail. If you want to make balance easier, put your forward foot on the daggerboard at the well.

69 | Sail 180 on the rail

As mentioned before, the term 'sail 180' means to spin the sail around 180°. It applies whichever direction the sail is pivoted, whether you start in clew-first orientation or in normal sailing orientation. In this sequence the sail 180 is performed by sailing clew-first, then letting the clew swing to leeward.

Ideal conditions for learning are flat water and a steady eight to 10 knot wind. Balancing as the sail swings around is made difficult by the sudden release of wind pressure as you let go with the clew hand, followed by an increase in pressure when you sheet in again. To get used to this sensation before trying the sail 180, sail along on the rail repeatedly luffing and sheeting in.

4/Keep the mast upright as the sail swings around. Some people prefer to hold the mast in both hands. The clew mustn't hit the water.

2/Transfer your rear hand to the mast.

3/Release the boom with your forward (clew) hand, allowing the clew to swing to leeward.

5/Change hands on the mast.

6/When the other boom is within reach, grasp it with your sheet hand and sheet in normally on the rail.

70 Riding the lee rail

A leeward railride is possible in light or strong wind because it relies primarily on balance unaided by the wind. However, wind of about eight knots is most comfortable for learning.

This move is easier if you commit yourself to raising the rail quickly. As you raise the rail, keep your body vertical and hold the rig vertical or leaning very slightly to leeward. For maximum stability, raise the board beyond vertical and tip it slightly to windward, so the rail touches the mast.

Troubleshooting

☐ If you keep falling to windward when the rail comes in

contact with the mast, try leaning the mast slightly more to leeward, so the board doesn't tilt so far to windward.

☐ A leeward railride calls for delicate balance. If you begin falling backward (to windward), right yourself by sheeting in to give yourself more power, and at

71 Stationary luff on the lee rail

This is a move you can perform for a moment to earn extra points in competition. It bears little resemblance to the previous stationary railride. In the sequence shown here, the luff is performed on a stern-first railride, but it can be performed in the same way sailing forward.

Turn the board toward the wind until you can spill air from the sail without having to lean off the rail. As the board heads up and slows down, set it perfectly vertical (remember, the hull is tilted slightly to windward for a lee railride). Luff the sail totally, so the board stops moving, and use steady pressure to hold rail and mast in contact.

the same time lean the mast slightly away from you (to leeward). Should the board begin falling to leeward there's nothing much you can do; unlike a windward railride, the mast has no leverage against the rail.

1/Sail on a beam reach. Stand well aft, where there'll be plenty of room for your feet under the sail when the rail is up, and hang much of your weight downward on the rig. Now, push the windward rail down with your forward foot.

2/As the lee rail rises, hook the arch of your rear foot over it and pull the rail up to touch the mast.

3/Before the windward foot slips off the sinking rail, transfer your weight partially to the foot you've hooked over the rising rail and partially to the boom, then get both feet onto the rail. Transferring weight like this requires committing yourself to raising the rail as quickly as possible.

4/Stand vertically over the rail, leaning the mast slightly to leeward.

72 | Clew-first leeward railride

Sail clew-first on a beam reach. Push the windward rail down with your windward foot, then hook the arch of the other foot over the lee rail and raise the rail to touch the mast. It's important to hold the mast vertical, or leaning slightly to leeward, so the board tilts at the proper angle when it makes contact with the mast.

When the rail touches the mast, transfer some of your weight onto the foot hooked over the rail. Hang the rest of your weight on the boom, and lift the other foot onto the rail.

Spin on the rail seen from windward. *This stage occurs between
the two frames taken from leeward.*

73 | Spin on the rail

*Gary Eversole initiates this spin on the lee rail by turning
toward the bow. Rather than make a continuous spin
he breaks the move into two parts, stepping one foot
around the other for each half turn.*

*First, perform a lee railride and position the board on
a close reach. Be sure the board is vertical and that you
stand directly over the rail.*

The first half turn

*Turn the forward foot to lie along the rail, toes pointing
forward. Luff slightly and slide the rear hand forward to*

*the balance point of the boom. Release the boom with
the forward hand as you turn your body forward. Then
step the rear foot forward of the other, placing it at right
angles across the rail, and quickly swing the forward
hand around to grab the boom behind your back.*

The final half turn

*Turn the rear foot so the toes face the stern. Twist your
body around before moving your feet, then swing the forward hand around your body and put it aft on the boom.
Complete the turn by stepping the forward foot aft.*

**1/First half turn seen from leeward. *Foot movements
are crucial. First, set the forward foot along the rail
facing the bow. Then step the rear foot in front of the
other, setting it down at right angles to the rail.***

**2/Beginning of the second half turn seen from lee-
ward. *Turning his right (rear) foot so the toes face
the stern, Gary twists his body ahead of his feet in
order to reach around and get his left hand aft on the
boom. With the left hand on the boom he'll step his
left foot aft and complete the turn.***

74 | Neckhold on the lee rail

Near the beginning of the book we illustrated a neckhold. Like many other tricks this can be combined with a railride.

Lift the lee rail using the technique already described. Hold the mast in your forward hand. Then bend your knees, pull the boom over your head, and use your neck to support the boom instead of the rear hand.

This position is recommended only in light wind, and even then not for long. When ready to move on, either duck your head out, or put your rear hand inside the boom and hold it, palm facing the wind, while you stand up inside the boom as described in trick 75.

75 | Inside the boom on the lee rail

Sail on a close reach and do a leeward railride. Hold the mast with your forward hand. Luff slightly, then duck your head and shoulders inside the boom. Hold the boom with your shoulders while slipping the rear hand inside the boom, palm facing the wind. Then hold the boom with the rear hand as you stand up.

76 | Lee-rail rollover

When a leeward railride is performed on a very broad reach, the mast can be leaned far enough to windward for the board to roll upside down. This is a lee-rail rollover. At first glance it looks like an everoll (see trick 77),

2/Gradually lean the mast to windward, shifting your hands nearer the clew, to let the board roll upside down. If you aren't far enough off the wind when you lean the mast to windward, the sail will backwind and blow over you.

1/Ride the lee rail on a very broad reach.

77 | Everoll

The everoll, one of many Eversole innovations, involves sailing the board upside down with the sail clew-first. The bottom of a sailboard is usually slippery, so if you don't use your board for racing, consider roughening the bottom or applying some nonskid substance. Alternatively, use footwear that grips extremely well.

This move is a potential mast-breaker, so reinforce the lower end of your mast thoroughly.

One method of doing the everoll is to sail clew-first on a beam reach, then flip the windward rail up and let it roll over to touch the mast. Since the mast usually leans off to leeward when you sail clew-first, the board tilts beyond vertical and you're in the first stage of an everoll.

Next, reach back along the boom, leaning the mast nearer the water to allow the board to roll farther over. As it rolls, step one foot and then the other onto the underside. To avoid putting excess pressure on the mast, keep your feet on the side of the board's midline that is opposite to the mast.

Sheet out slightly if you want to lay the board flatter on the water. Since the rig leans out over the water it exerts more leverage than you're accustomed to, and you'll have to counter by leaning back to stop it pulling you over. At times, you may even have to release the

boom with one hand to avoid being overbalanced. In this context, a high-clew sail makes an everoll harder by putting the boom further away.

Steering an everoll

If you lay the board flatter on the water it turns upwind. Lifting the rail slightly allows the board to be turned downwind.

but isn't because the sail isn't in clew-first orientation. It's possible to transform this into an everoll by gybing the hull, then turning upwind clew-first on the new tack.

3/Having rolled the board over, avoid putting weight on the side of the board that leans on the mast or you'll break the mast. Notice how most of Gary's weight is on his leeward foot (here, the right foot), which he places on the opposite side of the board's midline from the mast. Though his left foot is hooked over the windward rail to stop himself slipping, he puts little weight on that side of the board.

1/Sail on a broad reach and initiate a gybe by leaning the mast to windward and pushing the windward rail down.

2/As the lee rail rises, hook your foot over it and help it up. Meanwhile, slide your hands along the boom nearer the clew and continue tilting the mast to windward.

78 | Gybing everoll

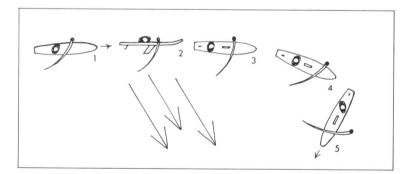

You've probably noticed that when you gybe using a full-size dagger-board in wind of eight to 10 knots or more, the sailboard tries to rise onto its rail, or rail-up. To stay on the board you have to luff, slow down a bit, and push the rail down with your feet.

For a gybing everoll you actually help the board rail-up as you gybe, then roll it upside down and stand on the underside as you head up, clew-first, on the new tack.

When you're practicing, 10 knots of wind is ideal.

5/The next stage is to turn the board onto the new tack. To do this it's critical that you grip the boom as near the clew as you can and lean the mast as far forward as you can. Next, step aft on the board and kick the tail around, through the wind. Then head up on the new tack, clew-first, and you're performing an everoll.

3/As the rail reaches vertical, step both feet onto it, then allow the board to roll over, stepping one foot at a time onto the underside.

4/The hull can only tip over as far as the mast allows, so reach farther back on the boom and drop the mast closer to the water until the board is totally upside down. At this point the sail is by the lee or very close to it, and if you aren't pointing low enough it will backwind and blow over you.

79 | Spin on an everoll, clew-first railride, then sail 180 on the rail

Strive for a smooth and graceful flow when you link these moves. Each has already been covered individually, except that here the everoll is performed stern first instead of forward.

The first frame here follows on from the final frame of sequence 82 (forward railride, reverse to stern-first everoll), which provides one of the easier ways into a stern-first everoll.

Frames 1-3: spin on a stern-first everoll

1/Gary kicks the nose of a stern-first everoll around to turn the stern upwind until on a beam reach.

Frames 4-6: clew-first, stern-first railride

4/Gary sets the board on the rail using primarily his feet, and using the mast only very lightly. As he raises the mast he moves his hands along the boom. Study frame 4 and you'll see how he uses his windward foot to push down the side of the board opposite the mast, then hooks the other foot over the rising rail to pull it up and support his weight.

5/A stern-first railride quickly turns away from the wind, as the change in angle between frames 5 and 6 shows. Therefore prepare yourself for the sail 180 before balance becomes excessively difficult.

2/Luffing, he holds the foot of the sail and passes it from hand to hand as he spins.

3/He pulls the rig toward himself in order to get both hands on the boom.

Frames 6-7: sail 180

6/To flip the sail around, Gary places the nearest hand on the mast, then lets go with the clew hand, allowing the clew to blow to leeward into position 7.

7/Changing hands on the mast, Gary pulls it to leeward as the sail flies around, then sheets in normally on a stern-first railride.

1/Ride the windward rail stern-first at 90° to the wind.

Reversing direction on the rail

The final maneuvers all involve reversing direction on the rail by rotating the rig to reverse the direction of its driving force. For example, while beam reaching on a stern-first windward railride you could oversheet the sail and pull the clew around over the other side of the board, so that you sail forward, clew-first, on a beam reach as shown in sequence 80.

Many other types of reverse are possible, depending on factors such as the point of sail at which you reverse, whether you pull the clew to windward, or start clew-first and let it swing to leeward, and what you do with the board after reversing.

80 Stern-first railride, reverse to forward clew-first railride

This reverse is carried out by oversheeting the sail and pulling the clew around to windward, into clew-first orientation. It's described for a stern-first railride, but the same technique works for a forward railride.

It's best to reverse direction when the board is at 90° to the wind, when balance isn't unduly difficult in either direction. If you find yourself overbalancing after the reverse, you could roll the board upside down into an everoll, as shown in sequence 82.

2/Before the board turns further downwind, over-sheet the sail and walk the rail toward the dagger-board, stopping between mast-foot and daggerboard.

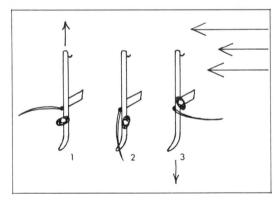

3/Pivot your body to face the bow, and pull the clew around over the windward side of the board into clew-first orientation. This reverses the direction the board sails in. While pivoting, keep your weight hanging vertically down on the rig.

1-3/Gary Eversole walks sternward on a stern-first railride.

81 | Sternwalk reverse

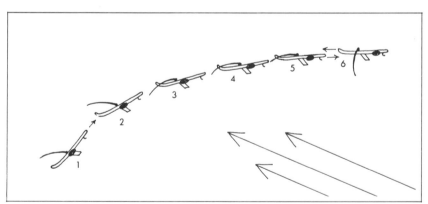

In this sequence Gary Eversole walks to the stern while doing a stern-first railride, sinks the tail in order to head up, then oversheets and pulls the clew around over the other side of the board to reverse direction. Since a stern-first railride turns downwind there will often be times when you want to turn toward the wind before reversing.

5-6/Gary pivots his body to face the bow and pulls the clew around over the other side of the board, thus reversing direction.

4/He sinks the tail, luffing to slow
down and maintain balance.

82 Forward railride, reverse to stern-first everoll

In this sequence Gary does a nose sink on a forward railride to turn into the wind. When head-to-wind he reverses direction by oversheeting the sail, and rolls the board upside down into a stern-first everoll.

It's interesting to follow the wake through the photosequence and see how lifting the stern from the water allows the force in the sail to swing the stern downwind.

This reverse was performed as the lead-in to sequence 79, which follows directly on from frame 4.

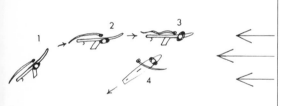

2. The board turns into the wind as the nose sinks.

1. Do a forward windward railride and step forward of the mast to sink the nose.

3. The moment the board stops moving forward shift your hands nearer the clew and drop the mast nearer the water to roll the board over. As it rolls, pivot your body to face the stern and put one foot on the underside, leaving the other foot hooked over the rail as shown. Notice how Gary carefully places most of his weight on the side of the board's midline opposite to the mast, to avoid levering the rail down onto the mast.

4. From position 3 Gary moves his hands back along the boom to tilt the mast closer to the water and turn the board further over into position 4. As the board rolls flat, Gary pulls the clew to windward into clew-first orientation, then kicks the stern around to turn the everoll upwind to a beam reach.

3/Sheet in as the board turns into the wind.

2/Push down on the nose to sink it, causing the board to head up.

83 | Bodyhang nosewalk reverse

This maneuver is similar to sequence 82 in that Gary Eversole does a nose sink to steer a windward railride head-to-wind, then reverses direction and sails stern first downwind. However, instead of rolling the board upside down into an everoll he drops it down right side up. Another difference is the use of a bodyhang nosewalk to turn upwind. In the bodyhang nosewalk, Gary hangs his weight on the rig to lower his body near the water, then walks his feet forward along the rail, leaving his body aft.

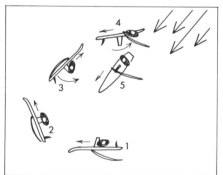

1/Perform a standard windward railride. Bend your knees and hang your weight on the rig, lowering your body near the water. Walk your feet forward along the rail, without moving the rig or your torso forward.

4/When the board is head-to-wind, pull the clew around to windward so you sail downwind stern-first.

5/Drop the board down right side up. Immediately sink the nose to lift the skeg clear of the water, so it doesn't catch and turn the stern into the wind.

84 | Clew-first stern-first railride, reverse to standard forward railride

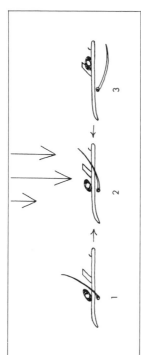

The reverses described up to now have involved starting with the sail in its normal orientation (mast first), then oversheeting so you end up clew-first or running. Sequence 84 shows the opposite process: starting clew-first, Gary reverses direction by letting the clew blow to leeward until it's in normal orientation.

Whether you start with the board sailing backward or forward, the technique is essentially the same.

1/ Do a stern-first clew-first railride on a beam reach.

2/ Walk toward the stern and pivot your body to let the clew swing to leeward until it's over the other side of the hull, thus reversing direction.

3/ Having reversed, you'll be on a standard forward railride.

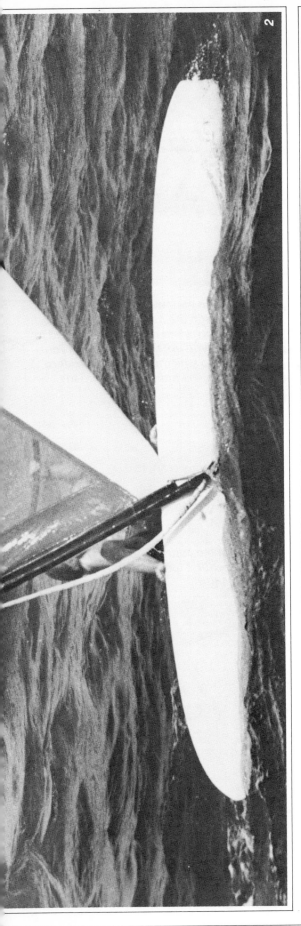

2/With your weight acting down through the mast to the mast step, so you're not relying on the wind to hold you up, push down with your feet to sink the stern. As the stern sinks, the hull turns toward the wind.

1/Perform a stern-first railride and put both feet on the rail. Hang your weight downward on the rig and, not changing the position of the rest of your body, walk your feet along the rail toward the stern.

85 | Stern-first railride, reverse to forward everoll, then clew-first railride

9/Make yourself comfortable on a clew-first forward windward railride.

This sequence joins five moves, each flowing naturally to the next. Gary starts with a stern-first railride, then does a bodyhang nosewalk to turn upwind (1-2). Oversheeting, he pulls the clew around until it's to windward of the hull, thus reversing direction (3-4), then rolls the board upside down into an everoll (5-6). Heading up on the everoll, he sets the board on to a clew-first railride (7-9).

Reversing direction on a railride in order to get to an everoll sounds complicated, but is actually one of the easier ways to do an everoll.

3/Pivot to face the bow as you pull the clew around to windward into clew-first orientation, thereby reversing direction.

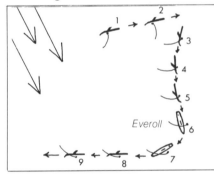

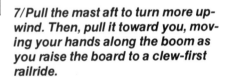

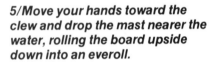

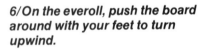

8/Hook the arch of your rear foot over the rail to pull the rail up, and transfer the other foot onto the daggerboard for maximum stability.

4/When in the stopped position, keep your weight over the board, perhaps with part of your weight acting down through the rig to the mast step.

5/Move your hands toward the clew and drop the mast nearer the water, rolling the board upside down into an everoll.

6/On the everoll, push the board around with your feet to turn upwind.

7/Pull the mast aft to turn more upwind. Then, pull it toward you, moving your hands along the boom as you raise the board to a clew-first railride.

86 | Tack on rail, reverse to everoll

3/When the board is on the new tack, backwind the sail, completing the tack on the rail.

2/Tack the hull by oversheeting the sail.

For the final sequence, Gary tacks on a standard windward railride, then reverses direction and rolls the board upside down, following this by gybing into a stern-first everoll.

Once on a stern-first everoll you can change to a forward everoll fairly easily. Turn upwind until on a beam reach, then luff, duck under the foot of the sail, grab the new boom and sheet in to sail forward.

1/Turn a standard windward railride into the wind.

4/To reach position 4 from position 3, step toward the bow, pulling the clew around to leeward as you move, and slide your hands nearer the clew to let the board tip upside down. As the board reverses direction and tips over, you may have to release the boom with your mast hand so that the mast can blow around to leeward without pulling you over.

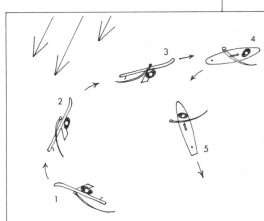

5/In frames 4 and 5, Gary gybes by scooping the wind and pushing with his feet. The flatter the board lies on the water, the more easily it turns upwind.

GLOSSARY

Aft: used here exclusively to mean opposite or away from the direction of travel

Apparent Wind: the wind a sailor perceives; the combined effect of the true wind and the wind caused by the board's travel through the water

Back-to-Back: with your back to the sail's lee side

Back-to-Front: with your back to the windward side of the sail

Backwind: (also BACKFILL) push the sail away so it fills on the side opposite you

Balance Point of Boom: point on the boom where forces on either side are in balance; a rig can be held with one hand at the balance point and it will not be pulled either way

Beam Reach: course or heading at 90° to the apparent wind

Bear Away: (also BEAR OFF) turn away from the wind

Bow: front end of sailboard; nose; end pointing in the direction of travel when sailing normally

Broad Reach: course between dead downwind and 90° to the apparent wind

Center of Effort: point on the sail through which all forces can be considered to act

Clew-First: with clew of sail nearest the wind, so that the mast becomes the trailing edge

Clew Hand: hand nearest clew

Clew Power-Through: technique used to push the clew through the eye of the wind

Close-Hauled: sailing as near as possible to the wind (about 45°)

Close Reach: course between close-hauled and 90° to the wind

Dead Downwind: course at 180° to the apparent wind

Everoll: sailing clew-first while standing on the underside of the sailboard

Eye of the Wind: direction the wind is coming from

Flyaround: pivoting the rig by releasing the boom with the mast hand, so the mast flies to leeward

Forward: nearest or nearer the direction of travel; used often in context of 'forward foot' or 'forward hand'.

Head-to-Wind: bow pointing directly into the wind

Head Up: turn towards the wind (opp. BEAR AWAY)

Leeward: on or towards the sheltered side (opp. WINDWARD)

Luff: used here to mean let the sail out to spill some air and reduce sail pressure; letting the sail out until it shakes

Mast Hand: hand nearest the mast

Oversheet: pull the clew of the sail to windward, beyond normal sailing trim

Rear: farthest from the direction of travel, as in 'rear hand' and 'rear foot'

Rig: the unit comprised of the mast, sail and boom

Run: course dead downwind

Sail 180: turn the sail around approximately 180° so the direction of airflow reverses

Skeg: underwater fin at the stern of the sailboard

Skipper 360: in which the skipper turns himself around approximately 360°

Stern: back of the board; part which, when sailing normally, is behind—but in freestyle, anything goes

Windward: lying in the direction from which the wind blows (opp. LEEWARD)

Color photos:

Front cover: Charlie Lewis on the rail. Photo Alan Williams.

1/ Lisa Penfield: splits on the rail. Photo Alan Williams.

2/ Twice as much fun. Photo Alan Williams.

3/ Someone has to watch where we're going. Photo Alan Williams.

4/ Two on the rail. Photo Roger Jones.

5/ Neckhold. Photo Steve Wilkings.

6/ Backflip through the boom. Photo Steve Wilkings.

7/ Roxanne Bisson of Quebec: back-to-back splits. Photo David Nicholson.

8/ Mark Robinson. Photo Alan Williams.

9/ Tandem. Photo Alan Williams.

INDEX

CODA

To reiterate what I wrote at the beginning: this book is intended as a guide, not a definitive manual. Freestyle is open-ended and can never be completely described or summed-up. My aim has been to introduce some maneuvers and principles that can be built upon, and the book will be most successful if it leads beginners to experiment and have confidence. Try every maneuver that seems to have potential; see what you can develop.

Good luck!